SAUNDERS PHYSICAL ACTIVITIES SERIES

Edited by

MARYHELEN VANNIER, Ed.D.

Professor and Director, Women's Division
Department of Health and Physical Education
Southern Methodist University

and

HOLLIS F. FAIT, Ph.D.

Professor of Physical Education
School of Physical Education
University of Connecticut

ARCHERY

second edition

LORRAINE PSZCZOLA

Physical Education Division Chairperson
San Bernardino Valley College
San Bernardino, California

ILLUSTRATED BY JAMES BONNER

W. B. SAUNDERS COMPANY • PHILADELPHIA • LONDON • TORONTO

W. B. Saunders Company: West Washington Square
Philadelphia, PA 19105

1 St. Anne's Road
Eastbourne, East Sussex BN21 3UN, England

1 Goldthorne Avenue
Toronto, Ontario M8Z 5T9, Canada

Library of Congress Cataloging in Publication Data

Pszczola, Lorraine.

Archery.

(Saunders physical activities series)

Bibliography: p.

1. Archery.   I. Title.

GV1185.P77 1976   799.3'2   75-28798

ISBN 0-7216-7389-9

Archery   ISBN   0-7216-7389-9

Last digit is the print number: 9   8   7   6   5   4

Editors' Foreword

Every period of history, as well as every society, has its own profile. Our own world of the last third of the twentieth century is no different. Whenever we step back to look at ourselves, we can see excellences and failings, strengths and weaknesses, that are peculiarly ours.

One of our strengths as a nation is that we are a sports-loving people. Today more persons — and not just young people — are playing, watching, listening to, and reading about sports and games. Those who enjoy themselves most are the men and women who actually *play* the game: the "doers."

You are reading this book now for either of two very good reasons. First, you want to learn — whether in a class or on your own — how to play a sport well, and you need clear, easy-to-follow instructions to develop the special skills involved. If you want to be a successful player, this book will be of much help to you.

Second, you may already have developed skill in this activity, but want to improve your performance through assessing your weaknesses and correcting your errors. You want to develop further the skills you have now and to learn and perfect additional ones. You realize that you will enjoy the activity even more if you know more about it.

In either case, this book can contribute greatly to your success. It offers "lessons" from a real professional: from an outstandingly successful coach, teacher, or performer. All the authors in the *Saunders Physical Activities Series* are experts and widely recognized in their specialized fields. Some have been members or coaches of teams of national prominence and Olympic fame.

This book, like the others in our Series, has been written to make it easy for you to help yourself to learn. The authors and the editors want you to become more self-motivated and to gain a greater understanding of, appreciation for, and proficiency in the exciting world of *movement*. All the activities described in this Series — sports, games, dance, body conditioning, and weight and figure control activities — require skillful, efficient movement. That's what physical activity is all about. Each book contains descriptions and helpful tips about the nature, value, and purpose of an activity, about the purchase and care of equipment, and about the fundamentals of each movement skill

v

involved. These books also tell you about common errors and how to avoid making them, about ways in which you can improve your performance, and about game rules and strategy, scoring, and special techniques. Above all, they should tell you how to get the most pleasure and benefit from the time you spend.

Our purpose is to make you a successful *participant* in this age of sports activities. If you are successful, you will participate often—and this will give you countless hours of creative and recreative fun. At the same time, you will become more physically fit.

"Physical fitness" is more than just a passing fad or a slogan. It is a condition of your body which determines how effectively you can perform your daily work and play and how well you can meet unexpected demands on your strength, your physical skills, and your endurance. How fit you are depends largely on your participation in vigorous physical activity. Of course no one sports activity can provide the kind of total workout of the body required to achieve optimal fitness; but participation with vigor in any activity makes a significant contribution to this total. Consequently, the activity you will learn through reading this book can be extremely helpful to you in developing and maintaining physical fitness now and throughout the years to come.

These physiological benefits of physical activity are important beyond question. Still, the pure pleasure of participation in physical activity will probably provide your strongest motivation. The activities taught in this Series are *fun*, and they provide a most satisfying kind of recreation for your leisure hours. Also they offer you great personal satisfaction in achieving success in skillful performance —in the realization that you are able to control your body and its movement and to develop its power and beauty. Further, there can be a real sense of fulfillment in besting a skilled opponent or in exceeding a goal you have set for yourself. Even when you fall short of such triumphs, you can still find satisfaction in the effort you have made to meet a challenge. By participating in sports you can gain greater respect for yourself, for others, and for "the rules of the game." Your skills in leadership and fellowship will be sharpened and improved. Last, but hardly least, you will make new friends among others who enjoy sports activities, both as participants and as spectators.

We know you're going to enjoy this book. We hope that it—and the others in our Series—will make you a more skillful and more enthusiastic performer in all the activities you undertake.

Good luck!

MARYHELEN VANNIER

HOLLIS FAIT

Contents

1

Archery as a Sport

Archery has come a long way since its first use 100,000 years ago as an invention for survival. Man first used tree branches and animal sinew to fashion bows and arrows; today he uses fiberglass, exotic woods, and aluminum. He was inefficient except at close distance, but today is superior at 100 yards. The bow was early man's necessity; today it is his pleasure. From its primitive crudeness to its modern ultrasophistication, archery has undergone many changes. Changes are still in progress. Recent introductions of refined aluminum arrows, plastic vanes, extension bowsights, and stabilizers are just part of the continuing growth and improvement which is taking place in this sport.

HISTORICAL BACKGROUND

The invention of the bow, the discovery of fire, the invention of the wheel, and the development of speech – all of these were fundamental in the civilization of man. The bow was man's first attempt at conserving energy. It enabled him to fight his predator from a distance; he was no longer forced into hand-to-hand combat for survival. Thus, the bow as a weapon elevated man above the beast.

The cave man used his bow and arrow to obtain food and to protect himself. Early bows have been found on all continents except Australia. They were involved in many aspects of man's life and history. From the Turkish short bow to the English long bow, and from the stubby Arabian arrow to the spearlike African arrow, archery has provided man with a weapon of survival, aggression, and defense. Military victories have been won by proficient bowmen for the Mongol hordes as well as for the English in famous battles at Crecy, Agincourt, and Poitiers. As archery became instrumental in maintaining man's way of life, bows and arrows became symbols. Cupid and his bow symbolized love; the huntress Diana was pictured with a bow; the bow became a religious symbol to the Zen Buddhists; and finally,

1

archery became a symbol of power as its representation appeared on the seal of the United States. It also became a symbol of historical romance through Robin Hood, whose feats with the bow made him a legendary hero.

No longer a weapon of survival, the bow today is an instrument of scientific perfection for a rapidly growing sport. Archery as a sport in the United States took root in the nineteenth century. With the establishment of the National Archery Association in 1879, archery grew in stature to encompass local, state, regional, and national tournaments. The International Federation of Archery (F.I.T.A.) now sponsors a world championship tournament every two years and archery is included in Olympic competition every four years. In 1970, there were reputed to be six million archery enthusiasts.[1]

NATURE OF THE SPORT

Emphasis in this book will be on archery as a competitive sport. However, for the sake of clarification, the games of archery as those forms which have a less competitive, strong recreational emphasis are presented. The games of archery are as follows:

Bowhunting and bowfishing. Specialized equipment is needed for these activities. A bow reel and a barbed arrow are needed for fishing, whereas heavier bows, broadhead arrows, and hunting sights are needed when going into the field.

Clout shooting. This is a form of long-distance (140 yards) shooting at a 48-foot target on the ground.

Archery-golf. This game is played on a golf course. One shoots with bow and arrow, while following closely the rules of golf.

Flight and foot archery. The object of these games is to propel an arrow as far as possible, using the arms in flight archery and the feet and arms in foot archery. The current records are 900 yards for flight shooting and 1100 yards for foot archery.

Roving. Roving is the shooting of arrows at various random objects (trees, bushes) on a cross-country course.

All of these recreational variations are interesting and fun to do. A good background in the sport of archery allows an archer greater success in any of these games.

The sport of target archery, the concern of this book, is a highly competitive activity which calls for the precise and accurate projection of the arrow each time the bow is released, using standardized rounds and distances. Although man has known the bow for most of history, the sport of using the bow is only now being recognized with the honors it deserves. Archery is one of the newest gold medal events

[1]Bert Bacharach: *Los Angeles Herald Examiner,* June 29, 1970.

added to the realm of Olympic sports. The revolution in archery equipment and shooting technique in the United States in the last 30 years made possible the elevation of the sport of archery to Olympic heights.

As with many other amateur sports, colleges could be the training ground for Olympic archers. The high schools could very well aid in the development of future Olympians because, as we survey the national scene, it is very evident that young people between the ages of 15 and 19 are among the champions. Archery is unique in that it has the shortest learning period of any other sport; it takes one to three years to develop an archer to the peak of his capacity, while it takes six to eight years to develop a swimmer, six to ten years to develop a tennis player, and up to twelve years to develop a gymnast. With the advantage of a short learning period, a high-school or collegiate archer could be trained and coached into Olympic prominence even though he had never shot a bow and arrow before this age. There are three prerequisites for archery success:

1. Good coaching
2. Good equipment
3. Personal qualifications of
    a. Highly developed kinesthetic sense, hand-eye coordination, and physical strength to draw enough bow pounds to be effective
    b. Patience, mental control through highly developed powers of concentration, perseverance in diligent practice, and desire to be a great archer.

BENEFITS AND ADVANTAGES

Archery is one of the fastest evolving sports today. The many changes in archery have brought about a sport easier to learn and more attractive to a great number of people. Archery has the following advantages over other comparable sports:

Archery is almost limitless in its capacity to be performed by both sexes and all ages. A child reaching the "age of reason" can be taught archery and continue to shoot safely for the remainder of his life.

Since there is little restriction in terms of sex and age, archery makes an ideal family recreational pursuit, joint hobby, and pastime.

Archery is adaptable to the individual's physical and emotional needs because a person can shoot with light or heavy bows, from short or long distances, and on small or large targets. Archery can be simple or complex to suit the abilities of the individual. Its flexibility makes archery appealing to many people.

The variation of archery (bird shooting, field shooting, target shooting) brings to it a cross section of the population.

Archery can be practiced on outdoor ranges, on indoor archery lanes, in open field space, or in one's own back yard. This variety makes archery a year-round sport even in the coldest climates. Indoor lanes offer league shooting in scratch or handicap contests.

Archery can be either a lifetime leisure activity or an intensly competitive sport. It offers the joy of craftsmanship in the making of bows and arrows as well as a realistic goal of Olympic achievement.

An archer can shoot by himself and be challenged only by his own scores or he can participate in archery club events, both social and competitive. Archery is an individual sport in its truest sense but can be a team effort in clubs and school.

Physical development takes place as a result of archery participation. There is walking for general exercise, and upper-body, shoulder, and arm development are a result of drawing and holding the bow.

The study of the history of archery can provide a challenging hobby to the archer. As mentioned previously, the bow has been in existence 100,000 years; this fact should be sufficient to whet the appetite of the toxophilite (student of archery).

One does not need to be in excellent physical condition in order to participate in archery, as proven by the many handicapped people who enjoy the use of the bow. Archery is included in the Wheelchair Olympics and is now being taught to the blind.[2]

The financial aspects of archery vary according to the means of the individual. An archer may spend as little as $8 for a complete set of tackle or as much as $350 for the ultimate in perfection and luxury.

Archery requires complete concentration. In this deep, quiet concentration an archer will find release and escape from the tensions and pressures caused by daily life. Archery can be a great form of relaxation for some people.

A short learning period allows the archer to develop to his maximum capability swiftly.

The personal satisfaction of deliberately and with total control aiming at and hitting an objective is great. Pride in accomplishment builds self-esteem and confidence. Here archery will not fail even the novice.

The dictates of any sport are established by the players at the highest levels of competition. The rules, techniques, equipment, and apparel are some of the dictates of archery. At world championship and Olympic levels the most talented archers test equipment for its accuracy, dependability, and total performance. The best equipment is then recommended for use. The rules of the sport are proven fair, stimulating to competition, and all-encompassing for control of the sport. Rules are first changed at these high levels of competition ac-

[2]J. Lavere Shaffer: "An Aiming Device for Teaching Archery to the Blind," *D.G.W.S. Archery Guide 1966–1968*, p. 29.

cording to the need. These rule changes are then accepted by the sportsmen in the country. Techniques of demonstrating skill are devised to encourage the best possible performance by the world championship archers and the best techniques are passed on to us. These continuous changes in archery equipment and techniques of shooting must be adopted if we are to maintain pace with the ever-improving performance records. The introduction of the fiberglass pole to track and field events and the uses of steel in tennis rackets and aluminum in arrows have had tremendous impacts on their respective sports. Materials change the response and performance of the equipment and the athlete must, in turn, change his technique to accommodate the new material. This change is for better, more satisfying performance, and archers are urged to try stabilizers, finger slings, oblique stance, draw checks, kiss buttons, and so forth. It is in the spirit of accepting the challenge of the new that this book ventures forth. Notwithstanding the sophistication of equipment, it is the person who must draw the bow, physically hold back the weight of the bow, aim the arrow, and release the string with accuracy. Success with the bow and arrow will always essentially remain commensurate with the talents of the archer. There has never been a perfect archer—the challenge is to see how close to perfection we can get.

2

Archery Equipment

A wide variety of archery equipment, or tackle, is available in archery shops and sporting goods stores. To the novice, choosing equipment could be a problem because of the variety of pieces and accessories available and the spread in price range. A beginning archer needs only the basic equipment to get started, namely, a bow, six arrows, an armguard, a fingertab, and a bowsight. A starting set could be purchased for as little as $8 to $10.

BOWS

Bows are made from various materials, in many shapes, designs, lengths, and weights, and can be purchased for $5 to $275.

The most popular and common bow design today is the *working recurve*. The working recurve or some form of it can be found in bows of all price ranges. Fiberglass and wood are the materials used in

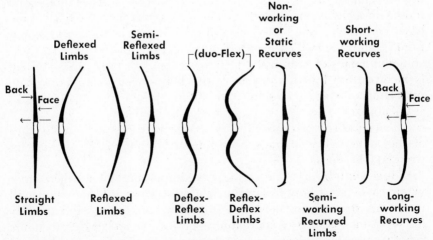

Bow designs. (From Phyllis Jacobsen: *DGWS Archery Guide 1964–1966*, p. 21.)

making bows. A bow made entirely of fiberglass or of fiberglass over a small wood core is the least expensive type. It makes an excellent beginner's bow, with the advantage of good durability. It will not warp or change shape due to storage or weather conditions and gives advance notice of weakening by the appearance of splinters on the surface. Wood is used in making the best and most expensive bows.

Layers of wood laminated into bow shape with a strip of fiberglass on either side of the bow makes up the *composite* bow. This type of bow has the combined advantages of both materials, that is, the smoothness of wood and the speed of fiberglass. When purchasing a bow, check for these qualities:

Smoothness in draw and release is necessary. Always shoot a bow before you buy it. The draw should be even and smooth from start to anchor point position. *Stacking* in a bow is not desirable, because most of the draw weight comes close to the anchor point position and is more difficult to hold and control. On the release, the bow should be smooth and should not "kick."

Recurved limbs should be a priority because of the added bow speed, or *cast*, provided. Cast is the speed with which a bow propels an arrow. The more cast a bow has, the greater performance we can expect of it.

The *riser* or center section of the bow should have weight (actual scale weight) which gives stability to the bow arm. The weight of the riser should equal the strength of the archer. Stability means less vibration in the bow arm during the aiming period and more control of the bow arm on the release. It gives an archer a feeling of solidity.

Stabilizers or some stabilizing features in the bow design will eliminate bow torque (left-right movement) and absorb some of the release shock. Stabilizers come in several forms. They are metal rods with weights on the ends which are screwed into the back of the bow. The single, long rod type stabilizer seems to be the most popular form. Mercury capsules inserted into the wood of the riser is a less common means of stabilization. In less expensive bows the stabilizer is incorporated into the design of the bow — what looks like ornate projections of wood on the top and bottom of the riser acts in actuality as a stabilizer.

The *length* of the bow will vary according to the needs and wishes of the archer. The average bow length for men is 69 inches, for women, 66 inches.

Bow poundage is one of the most important factors to consider when choosing a bow. An archer should choose a bow which will match his strength for holding a full draw comfortably and steadily for at least a six- to 10-second aiming period. An archer spends hours shooting in a tournament and he must repeatedly draw and hold. If his bow is too heavy, he will tire easily and will not be able to hold

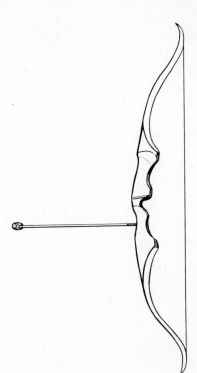

Bow with stabilizer.

his aim or control his bow, resulting in lower scores. For the champion, the last arrow of the tournament is as important as the first one, and if the bow is too heavy the archer cannot perform as well at the end of the day as at the beginning. Most people feel they can draw more weight than they are actually capable of drawing. Novices are particularly cautioned about using bows which are too heavy. Archers should learn to shoot with very light bows so that they are free to learn technique correctly without fighting against heavy weight. Average bow weights for the more experienced archer are: men, 34 to 42 pounds, and women, 24 to 29 pounds. The novice should try to use as light a bow as is available to him (15 to 25 pounds). Bow poundage is marked on the side of the bow, and is usually weighed at a 28-inch spread. If your arrows are less than 28 inches long, subtract 1¾ to two pounds per inch of draw less than 28 inches to determine the poundage you would actually be pulling. Likewise, if your arrows are longer than 28 inches, add 1¾ to two pounds per inch of draw beyond 28 inches for actual pulling weight.

Criteria for determining cast are as follows:

1. *Recurved limbs* — more recurve produces more cast.
2. *Bow weight* — more weight produces more cast.

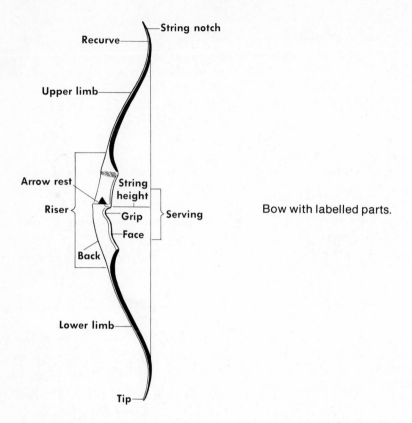

Bow with labelled parts.

3. *Arrow weight* — the lighter the arrow, the faster it flies.
4. *Amount of fletching* — smaller and fewer vanes allow greater speed.
5. *Degree of spiral fletch* — less spiraling allows greater speed.
6. *Diameter of arrow shaft* — smaller shaft allows greater speed.
7. *Closeness of arrow spine to bow weight* — balanced equipment performs better.
8. *Type of arrow rest* — smaller rest allows easier, faster take-off.
9. *Method of release* — action release produces more cast than a dead release.
10. *Use of fiberglass* — adds speed.
11. *String height* — higher string height conserves more energy.
12. *Grip position* — heeling the bow sends arrow higher than does holding it in the web of hand.

ARROWS

The length of arrows that an archer uses is directly related to the length of his arms. Correct arrow length can be determined by extending the arms at shoulder height and measuring from finger tips to

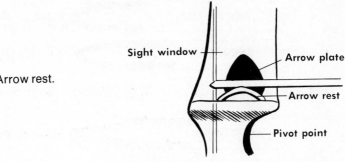

Arrow rest.

Sight window

Arrow plate

Arrow rest

Pivot point

finger tips. The chart is then followed to find the length of arrow that one should use.

Another way of measuring for correct length of arrows is to stretch the arms in front of the body with palms together. A yardstick is then held at the breastbone and measurement taken from chest to finger tips. The finger tips will touch the yardstick at the number indicating the length of arrow needed by that archer.

Arrows are made of three different types of material: wood, fiberglass, and aluminum. Wood arrows are the least expensive available and come in two qualities. Matched woods are those sets of arrows that are identical in weight and spine to each other. The weight referred to is the actual gram weight on the scale; spine refers to the flexibility of the arrow. For example, compare matchstick flexibility to oak-dowel flexibility. Arrows must be spined to match the weight of the bow from which they will be shot. If they are not matched to the

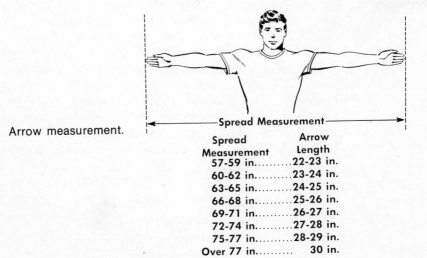

Arrow measurement.

Spread Measurement

Spread Measurement	Arrow Length
57-59 in.	22-23 in.
60-62 in.	23-24 in.
63-65 in.	24-25 in.
66-68 in.	25-26 in.
69-71 in.	26-27 in.
72-74 in.	27-28 in.
75-77 in.	28-29 in.
Over 77 in.	30 in.

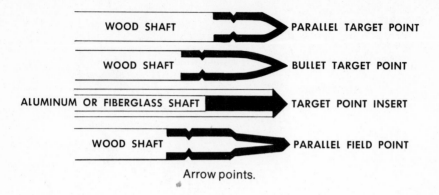

Arrow points.

bow, the flight will be unbalanced, erratic, and erroneous. Unmatched woods are those in which the arrows in the set are not identical. Wood arrows range in price from $4 to $14 per dozen. The main disadvantages of wood arrows are splintering and warping. Fiberglass arrows are very durable and are unaffected by dampness or temperature. The flight of a fiberglass arrow is much truer than that of a wood arrow because the former retains its straightness and the spine is more accurate. Fiberglass arrows range in price from $10 to $26, and they are preferred in the field. Aluminum is the best material for arrows since it can be manufactured to have a finer degree of flexibility and balance. The result is an arrow that flies more accurately. Aluminum is almost indestructible and is impervious to weather conditions. In international, national, and regional championships the best scores have been shot with aluminum arrows. These range in price from $18 to $46.

Fletching on the arrow comes in a variety of forms: some vanes are made of feathers and some of plastic; the shape of the vanes differs as well as their size; the manner in which they are applied to the shaft will also differ. The feather which is at right angles to the groove in the nock is called the *cock feather* and the other two are called *hen feathers*. The cock feather is placed away from the body of the bow in the nocking process, and most ordinarily is an odd color.

Feather size varies according to the size and weight of the arrow and determines how fast the arrow returns to straight-line flight after bending around the bow (archer's paradox). The smaller the feather, the faster it will return. The smaller feather is also more wind-resistant.

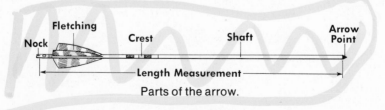

Parts of the arrow.

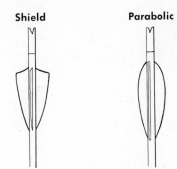

Shield   Parabolic

Feather shapes.

Feather shape determines the guiding ability and noise of the arrow in flight. Common cuts are *parabolic* and *shield*.

Feather spiral determines the rotation of the arrow in flight. The arrow must rotate in order to be stable. The heavier the tip of the arrow, the greater the spiral needed to keep the arrow balanced in flight. The number of fletch is a matter of preference, although most archers use three feathers or vanes, which is the minimum. More fletching adds to wind-resistance of the arrows but is less forgiving if the release hand is imperfect in performance. Plastic vanes are used by the best and most serious archers. They are wind- and weather-resistant and most reliable. The beginner is cautioned not to use plastic vanes because shooting technique must be mastered first in order to use plastic to advantage. The bow hand cannot twist (even slightly) toward the arrow on the release because this seriously affects the flight of the arrow by pushing against the plastic. Since plastic does not "give," as feathers do, the arrow is thrown off the target. Plastic vanes come in many sizes to accommodate the many sizes and weights of arrows.

BOWSIGHTS

A bowsight is a mechanical device attached to the bow which allows the archer to sight directly at and hit the target. A single pin setting bowsight is used for target shooting where distances are known. A multiple pin setting bowsight is used for hunting where distances are unknown. Bowsights are made of metal or molded plastic and range in price from $2 to $30 for simple sights and up to $90 for telescopic bowsights. Some qualities of a good bowsight are the following:

1. A small-enough aiming pin or aperture which allows good aiming.

2. A mechanism to lock elevation and wind positions independently of one another.

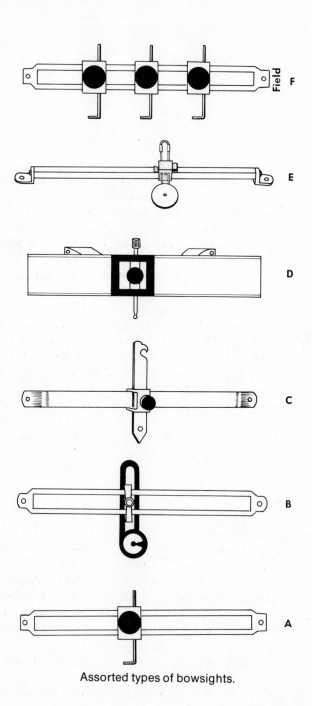

Assorted types of bowsights.

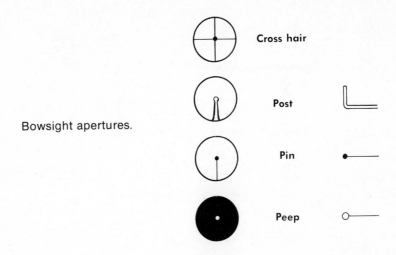

Bowsight apertures.

Cross hair

Post

Pin

Peep

3. A way of attaching the sight to the bow so that it will remain secure.

4. A place on the face or side of the bowsight to mark sight settings for all the distances that an archer needs.

Some bowsights are calibrated, some sit away from the bow on extension bars (extension sights), some have hoods over the aiming device, and some are prismatic. Bowsights vary to a great degree to suit the needs of many archers, and because there is a need for so many different types of bowsights, manufacturers are hesitant about putting sights on the bows they make. The archer should choose his bow and his bowsight independently. For the beginner, the wisest purchase in a bowsight is the least expensive one until he has had time to shop and test several others.

ARCHERY ACCESSORIES

Archery accessories can be categorized into essential, preferred, and "used as needed." The essential accessories are the armguard and fingertab or glove. The beginner is advised to purchase these when he purchases the bow and arrows.

The *armguard*, which is worn on the forearm, protects the bow arm against string slaps that may result in skin discoloration and stinging pain. The armguard gives the archer enough protection and security so that he can maintain a still bow arm on the release instead of flinching the arm away from the string. There is available a training armguard which is almost triple the length of a normal-size armguard. Used only in the initial stages of learning, the training armguard covers the bow arm from the wrist to two to three inches above the

Types of Armguards.

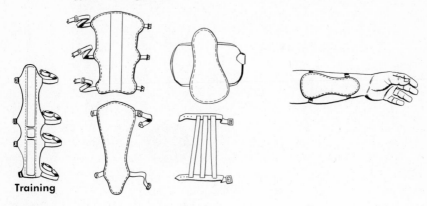

Training

Types of Finger Protection.

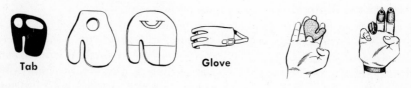

Tab

Glove

Types of Quivers.

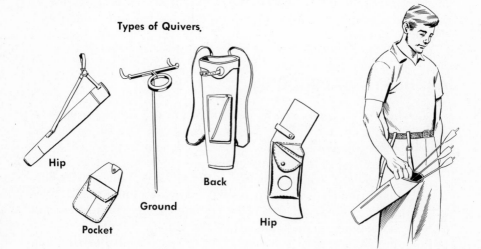

Hip

Pocket

Ground

Back

Hip

elbow. Armguards are made from plastic, leather, or aluminum, and vary in width from one inch to complete wrap around, in length from five to 15 inches, and in price from 80 cents to $4.

The *fingertab*, or glove, covers the middle three fingers of the drawing hand and offers protection against the force of the string. If a fingertab is not worn, the fingers become very sore and develop blisters, and the skin is liable to be cut. For ease in drawing, comfort in holding, and a smoother release, a fingertab is essential. These range in price from 25 cents to $2.50 and are made of leather.

In the preferred category of archery accessories are included quivers and finger or bow slings. A *quiver* is any device which holds arrows and other equipment for the archer during shooting. Aside from ground quivers, which are made of metal, quivers are made of leather or plastic. They vary from hip quivers, worn hanging from the waist, and back quivers, strapped onto the back of the archer, to pocket quivers, which hook onto the back pocket of a man's trousers. The price range for quivers is wide, from a small, plastic cloth hip quiver at $1.80 to a large hand-tooled leather one for $30 or more.

A *sling* is a device which keeps the bow under control in or near the archer's bow hand after the arrow is released. Good archery technique calls for a loose, relaxed bow hand. The sling allows the archer to relax by securing the bow to his hand. The bow sling is attached to the bow just below the grip, and the hand fits into a larger loop which rests on the archer's wrist. The finger sling is any device which can be attached to the index finger and thumb of the bow hand, with a crossbar of material between the two. Homemade finger slings are very ef-

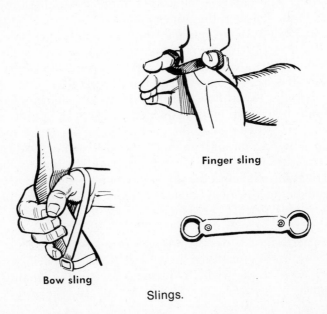

Finger sling

Bow sling

Slings.

fective. A leather strip with a slit at either end, or nylon cord with custom-made finger holes are two finger slings that are easy to make.

As the archer gains experience he may find need for additional accessories. Some of the "used as needed" accessories are draw checks, clickers, and "kiss" buttons.

BRACING THE BOW

There are several methods of bracing, or stringing, the bow. Bracing the bow is the act of bending the limbs and placing the loops of the string into the notches at either end of the bow. The use of a bracing instrument is the safest and best method for stringing the bow. One such device works on the principle of even pull pressure on the limbs by means of a single string attached to the limb tips. The string with small leather cups at either end, which is the bracing instrument, is held down with the foot while the hand pulls up on the bow grip. This hold-pull motion bends the limbs evenly while the archer slides the bowstring loop into the notch at the end of the bow. If a bow bracer is not available, bracing must be done manually. One of the manual methods of bracing is done by a push-pull movement on the bow. The string loop is set into the notch of the lower limb. That end of the bow is then placed into the instep of either foot with the back of the bow facing the archer. The archer then places one hand on the grip of the bow (same hand as foot instep); the other hand is placed on the upper limb with the thumb and index finger on either side of the loop of the string. The hand on the grip of the bow is pulled towards the body while the hand on the upper limb pushes away from the body. During the push-pull movement the fingers on the upper limb slide the loop of the string up and into the notch of the bow. The push and pull motions should be equal. Caution should be taken with recurved bows. When establishing the body position for bracing, keep the head and eyes to the side of the bow to avoid injury in case the hand on the upper limb should slip off the bow during the push motion. Until the bow is securely braced keep the pushing hand between the bow and your face. The step-through method is another manual way of bracing a bow. The archer steps between the string and the body of the bow so that his right hip is against the upper part of the riser section while the lower limb of the bow rests on his left ankle. The right arm then bends the upper limb, getting resistance from the hip, while the left hand moves the string loop into the notch of the bow. If this method of bracing is not performed correctly, it is very easy to exert uneven pressure on the bow limbs, resulting in twisted limbs. A twist in the limb results in loss of cast, which, in turn, lowers the quality of bow performance.

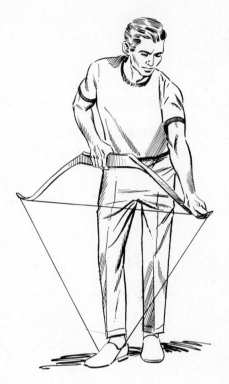

Bow bracer.

Manual bracing.

The use of a bracing instrument is recommended here because it is safe for the archer and at the same time will not allow limb-twisting to take place.

CARE OF ARCHERY EQUIPMENT

Good care given to archery equipment will prolong its life and performance, thereby adding to the dollar-value of the original purchase. In use and storage the basic rules of care are few and simple.

Bow Care

A cool, slightly humid room is an ideal place for storage of bows, which should be hung vertically on pegs or horizontally across pegs. Wood bows have added protection if stored in individual cases made of cloth or leather. The finish on the bow should be protected by an application of household wax to guard against scratches and moisture. Avoid leaving a wood bow on the ground because it can absorb moisture, resulting in warped limbs, and can be stepped on. The bowstring needs periodic waxing with beeswax in order to prolong its life.

Arrow Care

If wood arrows become wet while in use they should be dried off before storing. The best way to store arrows is in a case or box in

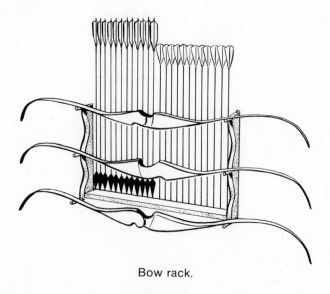

Bow rack.

which feathers and shafts are kept apart. Arrows should be carried by the tip ends, never by the feathered ends. If the feathers are damaged, the arrow cannot fly well, resulting in a loss of score. If arrows are to be stored for a long period of time (several months or more) the storage box should be moth-proofed to protect the feathers.

Leather Accessory Care

Leather goods can be cleaned, protected, and kept pliable by use of saddle soap. If leather gets wet, it should be allowed to dry slowly to prevent distortion in shape and cracking.

3

The Technique of Shooting

"Power," "beauty," "perfection," and "control" are some of the words used by observers at archery events. They describe an archer in action, for a champion is a picture of controlled power with movements that are graceful, precise, and perfectly timed. They are describing the technique of shooting: the devices and motions used by an archer which permit him to send each arrow to almost the same spot. Archery technique is composed of skills based on the scientific principles of physics, kinesiology, and anatomy. The steps necessary in shooting are very few when compared to the number of skills necessary to perform in other sports, but these archery skills must be completely mastered and perfected for good performance. At the outset of the learning process there is little room for individual differences; these come gradually as the basic techniques are learned to precision. The novice archer is advised to be patient and receptive for the first three or four lessons while he is acquiring enough skill to shoot arrows. The acquisition of new and unfamiliar skills can be difficult, but patience and determination will soon reward the beginner with the ability to hit the target face with each arrow from the shorter distances. The novice archer's acceptance of new information, along with practice time, will determine his learning rate and consequently his performance level. The initial learning yields a surprising amount of success, but as time and distances increase there is a slowdown in improvement and it seems that the archer cannot further his achievement. The archer should not be discouraged, for this familiar phenomenon is called a "plateau." After the steep climb to initial success, skill mastery in archery is made slowly by plateaus. To reach a plateau means the archer has mastered a certain amount of skill, and now he must start perfecting others or learning more advanced skills so that his performance level will slowly climb until he reaches the next plateau. By climbing from plateau to plateau the archer can reach championship heights. Each plateau should encourage the archer, not discourage him. He should congratulate himself for doing a good job, and then get to work on achieving the next plateau. The speed with which an archer moves from plateau to plateau is determined by his mastery of new skills as well as his motivation and desire for success.

The techniques of shooting a bow have changed over the recent years only as much as was necessitated by the changes in the bow itself. Archers have accommodated themselves to these changes in materials and design of archery equipment. Prime examples of this evolution were the introductions of fiberglass into bow construction and aluminum into arrow construction. As a result of fiberglass and aluminum, bow speed increased and arrows became lighter. Both of these factors made the arrow fly faster, making possible the use of a bowsight which is far superior to the point-of-aim method of aiming. The changes in equipment and technique continue even now, and archers must remain alert, ready to try the new.

Basic techniques of bow shooting can be categorized as stance, nock, draw, anchor, aim, release, and follow-through. Each part will be analyzed in detail with variations and innovations added. All references are made to right-handed archers. Reverse left-right directions for the left-handed archer.

STANCE

Stance is the position of the feet, the groundwork upon which shooting form is built. A good stance will give an archer the necessary balance and power he needs for drawing the bow. When choosing a stance the archer should consider several aspects to determine effectiveness. Does this stance give me a feeling of solidity? Does it allow my body to have a good alignment to the target? Does it encourage even weight distribution?

Two basic stances are the *square* and the *open*. The square stance is the traditional archer's foot position. The toes are on a line with each other and with the center of the target. The width of separation between the feet is a matter of preference, but less than shoulder width apart is not recommended. The weight is distributed equally on both feet and stays that way throughout the delivery of the arrow. Swaying or shifting weight to left or right or toward toes or heels will result in a weak foundation for the shooting form which must follow.

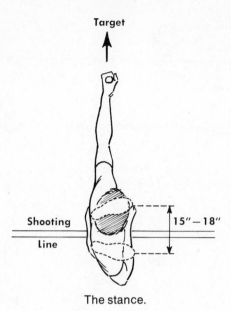

The stance.

The open stance permits the foot closest to the target to drop back several inches to allow for a more open body position. This stance is a little more difficult to master because the hip and shoulder closest to the target must follow in line with the foot which has moved back. It is not as natural a body position as the square stance. The advantage of the open stance is greater room allowance for the bow arm, which, in turn, gives the bow arm more stability. The advantage of the square stance is ease and alignment to the target. The archer should try both stances and decide which gives him the greater comfort, solidity, and balance in performance.

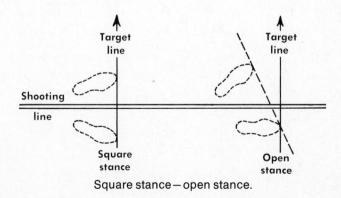

Square stance—open stance.

Full draw using square stance.

Full draw using open stance.

NOCK

Nock is the act of placing the arrow into the bow, followed by hand positioning on the string, in preparation for the draw. While holding the bow down at your side, parallel to the ground, with bowstring on the inside of the bow arm, place the arrow on top of the bow (left side when held in shooting position) with the cock feathers on the top. The string is fitted into the groove of the nock across from the arrow rest. In this position the arrow and string form a 90 degree angle. The nock of the arrow is then raised $1/16$ to $1/8$ of an inch. This spot on the string is called *nocking point* and anything used to mark the nocking point is called the *nock locator.* The nocking point of the arrow must remain constant with every arrow or there will be serious elevation differences in arrow placement. The nock locator can be made of additional serving thread wound to form a knot, or a felt pen mark on the string, or one of the many commercially made items of rubber, plastic, or metal. In order to be most effective, the nock locator should be of some height to offer resistance to the arrow nock and should be applied in such a way as to be immovable.

After the arrow is in place on the bow, the middle three fingers of the right hand are placed on the string in this manner: The index finger is placed above the nock while the other two fingers are placed below. The thumb should rest in the palm of the hand. The string is placed in the first joint line of these three fingers and *not* allowed to slip or roll forward to the finger pads. Some coaches advocate a deeper placement of the string, and there are some advantages for beginners in the use of this "deep hook." For a deeper hold, the string is placed between the first and second joints, or just the middle finger takes this

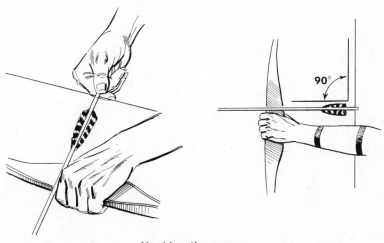

Nocking the arrow.

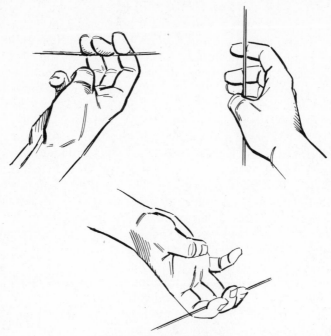

Hand position on string.

deeper position while the index and ring fingers keep the string in the first joints. In the deep hook all three fingers curl around the string more firmly than in the conventional position. The advantage of the deep hook is greater security for the beginner because the string cannot accidentally slip away. For this reason, the hold takes less conscious control. Both finger positions should be tried to determine which position offers the greater comfort, security, and ease in release. Both are accepted techniques and the archer should use that form which benefits him most.

Spreading the bow while using the correct muscles (upper arm,

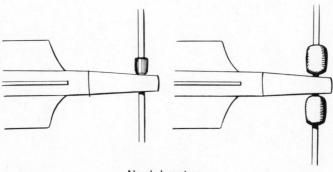

Nock locators.

shoulder, and upper back) is one of the most important factors contributing to successful archery. These muscles are the strongest available to the archer; and greater power allows for greater stability in draw and aim, allows use of greatest bow poundage and allows for the smoothest release. Instead of using this set of muscles (upper arm, shoulder, and back) a beginning archer might be tempted to use a combination of right hand and arm muscles to spread the bow, resulting in unsteadiness. When drawing the bow, you should feel the shoulder blades moving towards each other and the right elbow leading up and back. The correct proportion of push and pull while spreading the bow is also important. The left arm, while holding the bow away from the body, acts as a push force of stabilization as the major work in spreading the bow is performed by the pull motion of the right upper arm, shoulder, and back muscles. There are no scientific measurements to tell us the exact proportions of push to pull in drawing the bow, but it is advocated that the pull be greater than the push. The easiest way to learn to draw a bow correctly is by the use of a mimetic drill with a very light bow. A mimetic drill in archery is comparable to a dry land drill in swimming. It allows the archer an opportunity to learn the basic skill without the concern for and worry about success, because it is done without an arrow. A bow can be drawn safely without an arrow in it, providing the string is not released (this is further covered in the chapter on safety). Therefore, an archer can learn how to draw the bow with the correct muscles, anchor the string to the face, and aim with the bowsight without physical and psychological pressures. It is recommended that a new archer spend some time in drawing the bow without an arrow in order to develop good habits in drawing, holding, and aiming. Test your ability to hold a drawn bow aimed at the target without quivering. How long can you hold still? Some experts claim as long as 20 seconds.

Position of the right elbow.

DRAW

HOOK THEORY OF DRAW. Picture a man attempting to pull a heavy carcass of meat using a large steel hook. He puts the hook into the meat and, with the force of his arms, legs, and back, he pulls the carcass. Translated into archery terms, the steel hook is the right hand of the archer on the string. It is without power, a connector between the string and the back muscle. The back muscle is the "man" behind the hook which exerts the energy to pull. The steel hook does not pull the carcass of meat—the man does; the right hand does not pull the string—the back muscles do.

The act of drawing a bow is divided into three stages: the pre-draw, the primary draw, and the secondary draw. The *pre-draw* is the act of pointing the bow at the target with fingers on the string in readiness for drawing. In the pre-draw, the archer establishes the hand position on the grip and the left shoulder and left elbow positions.

The *grip* refers to the position of the left hand on the midsection of the bow. The bow itself is indented in the grip section of the bow handle and the grip center is the pivot point. The pivot is the balance point of the bow, where bow-hand pressure can be exerted most

Pre-draw position.

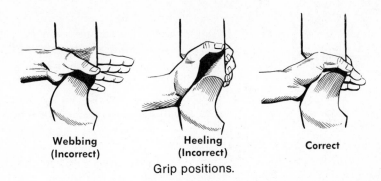

Webbing
(Incorrect)

Heeling
(Incorrect)

Correct

Grip positions.

effectively. If pressure is applied anywhere else, the bow will twist or kick on release, resulting in poor delivery of the arrow. The hand fits into the bow so that you can feel the bow down the "life line" of the palm. The left wrist is slightly cocked and sits directly behind the hand. Avoid rotation of the wrist to the right or to the left of the bow by keeping the center of the hand on the pivot point. A sideward rotation on the bow grip applies a one-sided pressure, which results in an unbalanced bow position when the string is released. The arrows will consequently fly to the side of the target face. An inward rotation of the wrist to the right of the bow will send the arrows to the left of the target face and, conversely, an outward rotation to the left will send arrows to the right. Even though most of the palm of the bow hand is in contact with the bow, the pressure is applied from the center and upper center of the hand only. For consistently good shooting it is essential to position the bow hand exactly the same way for each arrow, with pressure applied only on the pivot point of the bow. The fingers of the bow hand are relaxed with the thumb and index fingers acting as the control fingers by touching each other as they encircle the bow. The other three fingers are completely relaxed, and none of the fingers apply any pressure to any part of the bow.

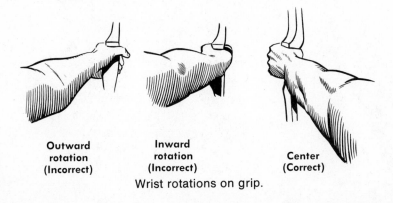

Outward
rotation
(Incorrect)

Inward
rotation
(Incorrect)

Center
(Correct)

Wrist rotations on grip.

The bow arm position is set and locked in place during the pre-draw. The ideal left shoulder placement is down and away from the string. This position can be achieved by keeping the shoulder blades together. A shoulder that is allowed to roll up and forward can interfere with the string path, resulting in bruises on the shoulder and poor arrow flight. Most often, the problem of the forward-positioned shoulder is caused by learning to shoot with a bow that is too heavy; this forces the archer to push the bow in too great a proportion to the pull. The open stance allows more hunching or rolling forward of the bow shoulder than does the square stance because hip and shoulder alignment is further back at the outset. The position of the bow shoulder is determined by the body structure, musculature, and strength of the archer, and is set and locked in place during the pre-draw. This position is maintained until the delivery of the arrow. The bow elbow should be as straight as possible without risking string slaps on the elbow bone or any part of the arm. The arm is extended with the elbow rotated down and back or to the left. Bending the elbow results in shakiness, and hyperextending results in pain and bruises. The elbow is locked in place during the pre-draw.

The *primary draw* is the act of spreading the bow from the pre-draw position to the anchor position on the face. The correct manner in which to draw the bow has already been covered in the general discussion of the draw. Beginners in archery have several common problems with the primary draw. The inability to fix the arrow on the arrow rest until the primary draw has been completed is a vexing problem to many archers. The possible causes for the arrows falling off the rest are (a) pinching the arrow nock between the index and large fingers of the right hand. This creates tension and pressure on the arrow which make it move. Put a pencil between these two fingers and press hard. You will note that the pencil moves in proportion to the pressure exerted upon it. If the nock of the arrow fits properly

Bow elbow position.

Correct   **Incorrect**

Draw check.

into the string you need not touch the arrow at all with your string fingers. (b) Using the finger and hand muscles to draw the string instead of the upper arm, shoulder, and back muscles. Hand tension results in arrow movement. The hand on the string should be flat, not cupped. Sometimes the rolling of the string onto the finger pads as it is being drawn forces the archer to create greater tension to keep from losing the string. (c) Drawing the string away (to the right) from the body, which forces the arrow to move to the left or off the arrow rest. The string should be drawn straight back to the face. Imagine that the string is moving back along your left arm; keep it close to your body. If the ring finger of the right hand is allowed to slip off the string partially or wholly during the draw or anchor, an unbalanced pressure on the string occurs that results in poor arrow flight. This fault is called "lazy third finger." Hook all three fingers equally on the string and keep string pressure equal on all three fingers throughout the shooting technique.

Draw check in archery means the archer's awareness of the position of the arrow tip in relation to the body of the bow at the end of the primary draw; his awareness of how much of the arrow he has drawn. The easiest way to perform a draw check is to watch the tip of the arrow at the end of the draw and to allow the tip to stop in exactly the same place each time the arrow is drawn. There are devices which, when attached to the bow, tell the archer he has drawn to his draw check position. These are clickers, mirrors, and so forth, and will be discussed under advanced techniques. A draw check is one of the skills performed by the archer which determine the elevation of the arrow. Consistency in good arrow patterns is not luck, but rather the performance of many skills during each draw that guarantee exact arrow position. The draw check is one of the more important skills that assure the archer that his performance will be consistent.

The *secondary draw* is a continuation of the primary draw. The primary draw ends at the anchor position, and the secondary draw starts there. It ends when the arrow is released. In the secondary draw the muscles of the upper arm and back maintain pull tension to keep the bow spread; to hold the primary draw in place; to maintain the draw check; to keep the archer from collapsing; and to keep the arrow from creeping forward. The secondary draw calls for more muscle strength than does the primary draw, since all of the bow poundage must be held back throughout the secondary draw. (In the primary draw there is a gradual buildup of poundage as the archer brings the string to his face.) During the secondary draw the archer aims the arrow. His muscles have locked into position so that no part is allowed to move, making the archer very steady and stable during this crucial phase of shooting.

ANCHOR

Anchor is the term which describes the position of the right hand and string on the face at the end of the primary draw. The anchor position is without question one of the most important factors contributing to success in archery. It ends the primary draw, secures the position of the back end of the arrow, determines the consistency of the sight picture, performs the task of a "rear sight," and allows the archer to see a string alignment to the bow. Consistency is the quality in an anchor position which determines its worth. Without consistency of performance, an anchor position is without value to the archer. We judge an anchor position by the number of contact points it allows an archer. If, in an anchor position, the archer can feel six points of contact between string, face, and hand, his position is better than one in which there are five points of contact. The more reference points an archer can use in establishing a position, the more consistent his performance will be. The anchor position which is most widely used and which is acclaimed as the most worthwhile is called the "low anchor" or "eastern." The string touches the center of the chin and tip of the nose (bisecting the face) while the right hand is placed under and touching the jawbone. This anchor position has three points of contact, and offers a greater number of contact points than any other known anchor. Placing the string precisely at the tip of the nose will assure the same head position for each draw; consequently, the position of the aiming eye in relation to the bowsight will be the same

Anchor position.

for each arrow. The sight picture (the string, bowsight, target) will be consistent with the correct performance of this anchor. The string hand is placed up against the underside of the jawbone. The top of the index finger of the right hand forms a shelf which fits up against the jawbone. The index finger is used in the anchor position because of its proximity to the nock of the arrow and its direct bearing on the position of the nock on the release. The three points of contact are (1) center of the chin with the string; (2) tip of the nose with the string; (3) hand under the jawbone. The use of the thumb in the anchor position has little or no value. Except for a very few unusual cases, the use of the thumb is not recommended because it can easily assume the contact place of the index finger, and perhaps allow the index finger to float. The index finger controls the back end of the arrow and if it is allowed to float the arrow flight will not be consistent. For most archers, the thumb should remain relaxed in the palm of the right hand. The string should be held firmly up against the face throughout the aiming period, locked in position by a firm secondary draw.

The cheek anchor in which the right hand is placed on the right cheek with the index finger in the corner of the mouth allows one contact point. The "western" anchor brings the string to the side of the face touching the corner of the mouth, while the hand is touching the jawbone just below. This anchor position allows two points of contact. In both these positions the string is to the right of the bow as seen in full draw, making good string alignment difficult.

AIM

To sight the bow accurately the archer must set his string in relation to the body of the bow (string alignment), aim the aperture at the middle of the gold (bowsight), and view the relationship of string, bowsight, and target (sight picture).

When using a bowsight an archer can sight with only one eye. A right-handed archer uses his right eye for aiming and a left-handed archer uses his left eye. Cross switching the eyes (right-handed archer using left eye) for aiming purposes in archery is not possible with to-day's equipment. Since the arrow and the bowsight are on the left side of the bow, the vision coming from the right side counterbalances. This aim allows the arrow to fly down the center toward the objective. Try this experiment the next time you are on the range. With sight and arrow in their proper places on the left side of the bow, aim with your left eye (instead of your right eye) and watch the arrow fly severely to the left, perhaps even hitting another target. Whether you keep both eyes open or close the left eye, be sure that the right eye is doing the aiming. If the right eye is non-functioning (blind or partially blind) the right-handed archer should learn to shoot left-handed so that he can use his left eye for aiming. It is much easier to aim correctly if the left eye is closed: greater visual concentration and fewer side distractions are possible. If a novice has difficulty in closing the left eye or in training the right eye to do the aiming exclusively, a patch over the left eye for the initial training period is suggested. After a few weeks the patch should be removed, since its use can later lead to bad habits such as peeking or flinching.

String alignment, sometimes referred to as string pattern, is the relationship of the string to the body of the bow as seen by the archer when in a full draw. The back end of the arrow must be positioned with the string; therefore uniformity in position of the string at the end of each draw is vital in producing consistency of arrow groupings. In a full draw position, with the string anchored to the nose and chin, the archer will see the string as a blurred, unclear line. This

Sight picture.

is due to the proximity of the string and the right eye. The ideal location for string alignment is the center of the bow. On a bow with a cut-out window the string is on the left edge. Some archers prefer the string aligned between the left edge of the bow and the bowsight. The boundaries of an acceptable string alignment position are from the center of the bow (on the right) to the sighting device (on the left). A beginner may have a tendency to pull the head back away from the string to get a clearer picture of the string. Acceptance of the blurred view of the string while it is touching the nose is essential in the correct performance of string aligning.

As soon as the string alignment is made with the right eye, the direct vision moves to the *bowsight*. While the direct vision is concerned with placing the aperture of the bowsight in the middle of the gold, the peripheral vision (side vision) keeps the string alignment in place. The approach to the gold by the bowsight from above, from below, or from the sides is incidental and left to the preference of the archer. The important part of the aiming technique is the steadiness and time of the bowsight in the gold. Aiming begins when the muscles steady down enough for the bowsight to stay within the confines of the gold. When the sight is in the middle of the middle of the middle, it is time to release the string.

The *sight picture*, as established by the archer, is as follows: (1) string alignment set, (2) bowsight in gold, (3) target in the background. The vision goes from the string alignment to the bowsight on the target and remains there until the arrow is released. Switching vision from string alignment to sight to target to sight, and perhaps back again for a quick check on the string alignment, will cause a strain on the eye muscle and will result in poor aiming. One theory states that the archer sees the target face clearly (long-distance vision) with bowsight and string alignment (close vision) as blurred, the other theory claims that the string alignment and sight are seen clearly on a less clear target. It is evident that the archer cannot see the target face and bowsight with the same clarity—the human eye does not have this capacity. A choice must be made as to which of these methods will be used when aiming. It is recommended that the latter method be used for greater control. If the close vision is used (the sight and string positions are clear on a slightly blurred target), the archer has a much better chance of controlling the windage (left-right dispersions) of his arrows through clear string alignment control. The sight picture must be the same for every arrow if the archer wishes arrow grouping on the target.

If, during the aim, you are dissatisfied with any aspect of the shot you should start all over. Whether you are undecided about releasing or are questioning the correctness of draw and anchor, it is better to let the bow down and start the shot all over than to flinch and lose an arrow. Once you have decided to release the arrow, aim as long as possible before releasing.

RELEASE

The act of releasing the string can be the most challenging of all archery techniques to master. A good release is one that gets the

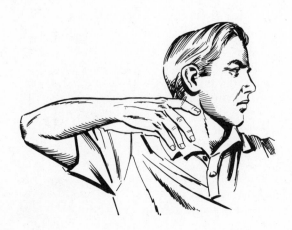

Release.

fingers off the string without ill effect on the arrow's flight or on bow control. Smoothness, balance, action, and timing are some of the criteria that determine a good release. When the eye sees a good sight picture the brain receives the message to release. The message is relayed to the back muscles which give a final squeeze at the same instant that the right fingers relax. If this act of releasing is performed as just described, the hand with relaxed fingers will move back along the neck as a result of back muscle action. If the hand muscles relax, the release will be smooth; if all three fingers relax at the same time the release will have balance; if the back muscles trigger the release, the path or action of the hand will be backward along the neck; and if the physical and mental coordination of the archer is good the release will be well-timed.

A release performed by the finger muscles, leaving the hand in the anchor position, is called a "dead release." Some archers have had some success with this type of release but the "action" or "live" release is recommended for greater consistency and tighter groupings. The novice should keep in mind that any movement of the fingers other than backwards in line with the nock end of the arrow will cause deviation in arrow flight. If the hand moves forward, or flies out to the right, or rotates inward to the neck, or snaps down toward the chest, the arrow cannot fly straight. All these release faults will send the arrow off its course.

FOLLOW-THROUGH

The final step in shooting an arrow is the follow-through, or hold, after the arrow has been released. Time must be given for the tail end of the arrow to clear the bow and for instant evaluation of performance. The bow arm is held at the same level after the release as before the release; the vision held on the gold; and the right hand fingers in contact with the neck. The archer's awareness of the location of these three parts of his body will give him the control necessary to give the final guidance to the arrow as it is sent out of the bow. During the follow-through the archer evaluates his entire performance in order to be able to repeat those parts that were done well and to eliminate those parts that were not. If the archer cuts short the follow-through, he doesn't give himself the chance to sort out the bad techniques and in a short time his bad habits will mount. Awareness of the good and bad in one's technique will foster rapid improvement in score. Shooting too fast with little or no follow-through does not give the archer the opportunity to analyze or "think through" the shot, but instead leads to a steady disintegration of technique and performance. Compare the follow-through to posing for a picture. Remain motionless after the release for three long counts and ask yourself, "Is the sight somewhere near the gold?" "Am I still aiming?" "Is my right hand on my neck?" To watch the arrow fly to the target is one of the most grievous faults in archery. The bow and head do not move at the instant of release or all is lost. CONCENTRATE – THINK.

Follow-through.

A composite archery technique list follows:

Stance
- Square Stance – Open Stance
- Equal distribution of weight
- Comfortable, solid, balanced

Nock
- Nocking point ⅛ inch above perpendicular
- Use a nock locator
- One finger above – two below arrow
- String in first joints of the fingers

Draw
- Use shoulder, back muscles
- Hand in pivot point of bow
- Rotate bow elbow
- Keep bow shoulder down
- Pre-draw, primary draw, secondary draw, draw check

Anchor
- String to nose and chin (bisect face)
- Hand under jawbone

Aim
- Use the right eye
- Check string alignment
- Keep bowsight in middle of the gold
- Consistent sight picture

Release
- Pull with back muscles
- Relax the right fingers
- Hand moves backwards
- Keep fingers in contact with neck

Follow-through
- Release hand still on neck
- Bow arm on target level, sight in gold
- Keep aiming
- Pose for a picture
- Analyze the shot
- THINK

Technique Analysis Chart

Technique	Error	Result
Stance		
Square stance		
1. Straddle the shooting line in a comfortable shoulder width stance. Feet, hips, and shoulders are in line.	Right hip and shoulders turning to face the target.	A change in body angle will vary distribution of arrows; mainly to the left.
2. The feet are parallel to the target with weight distributed equally.	Leaning into the target by placing weight on the left foot.	Arrows will land low on the target.
3. With the left side toward the target, only the head is turned to face the target.	Rocking side to side, thereby creating an unbalanced position.	A vertical dispersion of arrows (high and low).
Open stance		
1. The forward (target side) foot is about six inches behind the other foot, the toes are turned slightly towards the target.	Leaning away from the target by placing weight on the right foot.	Arrows will tend to land high on the target.
2. The hips and shoulders follow the position of the feet into a partially open stance.	Rocking forward and backward to create an unbalanced position.	A lateral dispersion of arrows (left and right).
	Weight on the heels of the feet.	Arrows mainly on left side of the target.
	Weight on the toes of the feet.	Arrows mainly on the right side of the target.
Nock		
1. While holding the bow on the left side of the body, place the arrow over the top of the bow.	Placing the string at the very ends of the fingertips.	Arrows will tend to fly left due to tension in the string hand.
2. The cock feather is placed up and away from the bow.	Placing the string into the fingers too deeply.	Arrows will tend to fly to the RIGHT.
3. Place the nock of the arrow into the serving of the string at right angles to the bow and then raise it ⅛ inch. Mark this nocking point.	Pinching the arrow nock between the fingers.	Arrow falls off the arrow rest, fingers become sore, development of blisters on inside of index finger and arrows will tend to fly to the LEFT.
4. Use the middle three fingers of the right hand on the string. Index finger is placed above the arrow nock; middle and ring fingers are below the nock. The thumb is relaxed in the palm of the hand.	Nocking the arrow in a different place for each shot.	A vertical dispersion of arrows.
5. String is placed in the first joints of these three fingers.	Nocking the arrow too high.	Arrows land low.
6. Always use a leather accessory on the string fingers for protection against skin damage and finger soreness.	Nocking the arrow too low.	Feather burns on the bow hand, wobbly flight of arrow tending to cluster high.
	Nocking the cock feather down.	Feather is crushed against the body of bow on the release; feather is damaged; erratic flight to the left.
	The thumb of the string hand on the back end of the nock.	Mis-nock might result with loss of score.

Technique Analysis Chart *(Continued)*

Technique	Error	Result
Draw		
Bow arm	Drawing less than usual.	Arrow lands low.
1. Hold the bow loosely in the left hand. Use the index finger and thumb as the control fingers as the bow rests in the center of the hand.	Drawing more than usual.	Arrow lands high.
2. Bow elbow is rotated backwards and away from the string.	Bow wrist too far right on grip.	Arrows will fly left.
3. Bow shoulder is down and back.	Bow wrist too far left on grip.	Arrows will fly right.
4. Primary draw: The pull which starts at the beginning of the draw and ends at the anchor position.	Heeling the bow.	Arrows will land high.
5. Secondary draw: The pull which starts at the anchor point and ends with the release. This is the action which keeps the primary draw in place and prevents creeping forward of the arrow.	Webbing the bow.	Arrows will land low.
6. Draw check: The arrow tip relationship to the body of the bow must be consistent with each shot.	Gripping the bow tightly.	Arrows tend to the left — tension causes lack of control.
	Hyperextension of the bow elbow.	Injury to elbow as the string passes; arrows fly low and left.
	Rotation of bow wrist into or away from bow.	Bow twist on the release. Loss of control.
	Bow elbow bent too much.	Lack of stability in drawing and aiming. Inconsistent flight pattern.
	Rotation of bow shoulder inward toward string (hunched shoulder).	Forces misalignment of body which causes arrow to fly left and string bruise on the left shoulder.
String arm	Drawing with the finger and hand muscles, resulting in a cupped hand.	Arrow will fall off arrow rest; rough release which will send arrows to the left.
1. The hand on the string is used as a hook with all effort of the draw originating from the back, shoulders, and upper arm muscles.		
2. The hand from the second joint knuckle to elbow should be in a straight line.	Using the hand and forearm to draw the bow, causing the string elbow to hug the chest.	Misalignment of body position; rough release which will send arrows to the left. Lack of stability and strength due to use of weaker muscles will send arrows low.
3. The string arm elbow is kept at the same elevation as the arrow or slightly higher as the string is brought to the face.		
4. The shoulder blades should move towards each other on the draw.		
5. An overdraw of the arrow should be avoided. This occurs when the tip of the arrow is drawn beyond the body of the bow.	Lazy third finger.	Blisters on index finger; string elbow out of alignment; arrows land high.
Anchor An anchor position, which is a string-hand-face relationship, is judged by the number of contact points it affords the archer. The more places the string touches the face of the archer the more consistency it allows the archer. The anchor position aims the nock end of the arrow and acts as a "rear sight."	Anchoring higher on the jawbone than usual.	Arrows will land lower than usual.
	Anchoring lower than the jawbone.	Arrows will land higher than usual.
	Use of the thumb as a hook under the jawbone.	Prevents a good release and will vary the elevation of the arrow pattern.

(Table continued on the following page.)

Technique Analysis Chart *(Continued)*

Technique	Error	Result
1. The string bisects the face, touching the chin and the tip of the nose, while the hand is placed under and in contact with the jawbone. The shelf of the hand (index finger) meets the underside of the jawbone.	Creeping forward of the arrow during the aiming period.	Arrows will vary in elevation, mostly low.
	Anchoring with mouth open. Teeth should be clenched.	Arrows will land high.
	Leaning head forward to meet the string hand.	Inconsistent amount of draw; arrows mainly low on the target.

Aim
1. Right-handed archer uses his right eye; left-handed archer uses his left eye. *Test for eye dominance:* With both eyes open point index finger on an object; by alternately closing eyes, the archer finds the eye which is closest to the finger on the object. This is the dominant eye.
2. Hold until the aiming device settles down in the center of the center of the center of the target. Hold breath during aim.
3. String alignment should be consistent with each shot. This is the string relationship to the bow as seen by the archer during the aiming period. The string should be close to the left side of the bow. The limits of a good string alignment are from the center of the bow to the bowsight.
4. Draw your preferred string alignment in the accompanying square.

Error	Result
Not holding the aim long enough.	Snap shooting with a wide scatter of arrows.
Disregard for string alignment.	Lateral dispersion of arrows.
Aiming with the wrong eye.	Arrows completely off the target to the left.
Vision switching from bow to sight to target and back again. Tired eye muscles will cause poor aiming.	Scattered arrow pattern on the target.
Inhaling just prior to release.	Arrows will land high.
Exhaling just prior to release.	Arrows will land low.

Release
1. With a force created by extra tension on the upper back muscle, the right hand rolls backward off the string with relaxed fingers.
2. The hand follows a path directly back of the arrow with fingers in contact with the neck.
3. Release movement ends when shoulder blades meet.
4. Left arm remains at same level as during the aiming stage. Left hand remains relaxed. Continue to aim after the arrow is released.
5. Short-sleeved, tight-fitting clothing should be worn so that nothing interferes with the string on the release.

Error	Result
Snapping off the string.	"Twanging" the string causes arrows to go to the left; sore fingers.
Releasing forward; all movement starting with the draw is backward.	Loss of bow power; arrows land low.
Tension in left hand or arm causing wrist or elbow to move toward string.	Bruises; arrows land low and left.
Bulky clothing worn in cold weather.	String "catches" on the obstructions; loss of bow power; arrows land low and left.

Technique Analysis Chart *(Continued)*

Technique	Error	Result
Release practice: With hooked fingers place hand into anchor position. Hook left fingers into right fingers and create a resistance to the anchor hand. The right hand can then mimic a release with opposition from the left hand.	Moving bow in any direction on the release.	Arrows are pushed off target line in the direction the bow is moved.
	Moving bow and head to watch the arrow.	"Peeking" causes arrows to land high and right.
	Flinching is bending the bow elbow on the release. This is usually done as a subconscious effort to protect an injured elbow.	Arrows land left on the target.
	Dead release.	Arrows fly low.
	Release fingers move inward to the neck instead of straight back.	Arrows land right on the target.
Follow-through 1. Hold the release position for at least three seconds. In this time period check two items: (a) Is the bowsight still on or near the gold? (bow control) (b) Are the release fingers still in contact with the neck? (good release) 2. *Pose* as for a picture.	Insufficient time spent on self-analysis.	Bad habits formed by repeating mistakes; shooting without awareness of cause and effect; poor archery.

4

The Use of the Bowsight

The most accurate aiming in archery is done with the bowsight. This device allows the archer to aim directly at the target, which gives a psychological advantage over the obsolete point-of-aim method of aiming. It is not possible to aim the tip of the arrow at the target and expect the arrow to hit that target from every distance. The reason for this is that the sight line and the flight line are not the same. The eye sees in a straight line, whereas the arrow flies in an arc. The bowsight allows the archer to aim directly at the target from every distance, and thereby negates the difference between the sight and flight lines. The bowsight is attached to either the back or the face of the bow, depending on the preference of the archer. A bowsight attached to the face of the bow allows a little more yardage than one on the back of the bow.

The position of the bowsight setting for each distance is found by trial. If the technique of the archer is good, a bowsight setting can be

Attached bowsight.

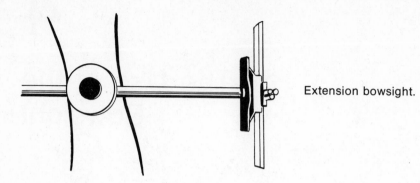

Extension bowsight.

Mark your bowsight settings for all the distances you need.

Example

1	
2	◯ 20 Yards
3	
4	◯ 30 Yards
5	
6	
7	
8	
9	
10	
11	
12	

1
2
3
4
5
6
7
8
9
10
11
12

Bowsight setting record.

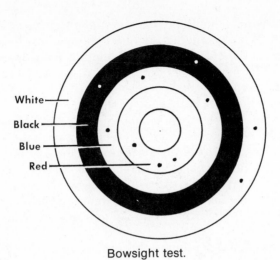

White
Black
Blue
Red

Bowsight test.

determined in a very few arrows. There are five major criteria determining a bowsight setting. The *height* of the archer is one factor since it determines the elevation of the bow when held in relation to the target. The *weight* of the bow will account for the cast, therefore the faster the arrow travels the higher on the target it will hit. The *length of the arrow* also determines a bowsight setting because the more distance the bow is spread, the more energy is stored and released. This energy or cast will determine the height of the arrow. The *distance from the target* is a major factor in placing the bowsight. The greater the distance from the target, the lower the bowsight is set. As a rule, we can equate 10 yards on the ground to 3/4 inch on the bowsight bar. For each 10 yards the archer moves away from the target, he lowers his sight 3/4 inch. *Weather,* particularly the humidity, determines the reaction of the bow and arrow materials. The wetter the air, the heavier the materials and the slower the reaction. A lower bowsight setting is used.

When attempting to establish a setting for a new yard line, or in a first attempt at using a bowsight, it is safer to set the bowsight too high rather than too low. In this manner the first arrow will not overshoot the target; instead, it will be low on the target or in the turf in front of the target and easier to find. Always aim the aperture of the bowsight at the center, or gold, of the target. As soon as some grouping of arrows occurs, move the bowsight for necessary adjustment in this way: If arrows group high, raise the bowsight. If arrows group low, lower the bowsight. If arrows group left, move bowsight to the left. If arrows group right, move bowsight to the right.

The bowsight should be moved a little at a time until you can aim at the center of the target and hit it fairly consistently. Once this place is found, its position should be marked on the sight bar for future use and reference. When changing the bowsight to adjust for variance in windage(left-right) hold the bow in shooting position, particularly if the bowsight is mounted on the back of the bow. To turn the bow around when making windage adjustments could easily result in an error (reversing the direction of the changes).

An extension bowsight works on the same principle as a bowsight mounted on the bow proper. The difference between these bowsights is that one is situated 8 to 12 inches in front of the bow and is attached to the bow by means of a bar of strong material, metal or heavy molded plastic. The advantage of the extension bowsight is that it forces more accurate aiming. The muscle and bow vibrations are magnified in an extended bowsight; the archer is forced to wait for settling-down and to aim more carefully.

As a project, mark your bowsight settings for all the distances you need. Test yourself on how well you know how to adjust a bowsight.

5

Safety and Injury Prevention in Archery

By its very nature the sport of archery is potentially dangerous. The bow is a weapon and can be deadly. This fact necessitates compliance with basic safety operating principles. Not only can injury of others be caused by the archer, but he can injure himself by the use of faulty equipment or incorrect shooting technique. Knowledge of safety procedures, awareness, safety consciousness, and good sense are prerequisites for a safe archer. The following suggested safety considerations are categorized into bow safety, arrow safety, range safety, and technique safety.

BOW SAFETY

When bracing a bow manually, keep the fingers on the top of the bow in order to avoid pinching them between the string and the bow. This is particularly important with a highly recurved bow. The hand should act as a shield between the bow and the face of the archer by remaining in contact with the bow until the bow is completely braced.

A bow is designed to bend in one direction. Care should be taken to brace it correctly in that direction only.

A bow should be checked often for splinters, cracks, and other defects. A damaged bow is more likely to break or explode and is most dangerous to use.

A bow which is drawn without an arrow should not be released. The manufacturer makes the bow to be drawn and released safely up to a certain number of inches. To overdraw the bow might create too much stress, causing the bow to break. Shoot only a real arrow from a bow, not an imaginary one. This is a good rule to remember.

A bow should be properly limbered. Several one-quarter to one-half draw length pulls done slowly and easily will warm up the bow. This procedure will minimize chances of the bow breaking by preventing sudden and complete stress to the fibers of the bow. Unused bows and those stored in warm, dry places need more time to warm up.

Check string height before each use. If the string height is too narrow, the archer will suffer string slaps on the bow wrist.

A worn bowstring should be changed before it breaks. The shock of a broken string very often breaks a bow.

Keepers are small strings which join the top of the bow to the top loop of the string. They should be in good condition—when a bow breaks the top limb may fly toward the archer.

ARROW SAFETY

Wood arrows should be checked often for splinters and cracks. It is extremely dangerous to shoot a damaged arrow. The defect creates a weakness in the shaft, which then cannot bear the thrust (power) of the bow. The arrow will shatter or explode upon release.

An arrow should not be drawn beyond the body of the bow. In this position the arrow may be released into the bow, causing the arrow to shatter or be driven into the bow hand.

It is safer to shoot with an arrow that is too long than one that is too short. An arrow that is too short will be overdrawn easily.

An arrow that is insufficiently spined for a bow might shatter from the force of the bow when it is released. All sporting goods stores carry spine charts for arrows.

While in a full draw, if an arrow falls off the arrow rest, do not attempt to replace it until you have brought the equipment down. It can be accidentally released into undirected flight if you attempt to correct the situation while in full draw.

Arrows should be carried at the tip ends in order to keep the feathered ends apart. Damaged feathers will not fly well.

If the arrow tip has been pushed into the shaft as a result of hitting a hard surface, file it down until smooth before shooting again. The splinters could damage the bow hand.

Check the base of the feathers for excess glue deposits. These should be sanded down to avoid cuts (feather burns) on the bow hand as the arrow passes on the release.

The nocking point for the arrow should be high enough to avoid feather burns, which occur when the arrow is nocked too low.

When not in use, arrows should be placed in a quiver rather than on the ground, where they could be slipped on or tripped over.

RANGE SAFETY

Archery equipment should be carried vertically as much as possible since in this position there is less chance of injuring other people. It is dangerous to run when carrying bows, arrows, quivers, and so forth.

A common shooting line should be used for group shooting. Each archer should straddle the line to insure safety to all other archers. The ideal range consists of one shooting line with targets placed at different distances.

Observe all whistle signals for shooting and retrieving: one blast for "shoot"; one blast for "retrieve"; double blast for "emergency — stop."

A nocked arrow is comparable to a loaded gun. Do not nock the arrow until the "shoot" whistle is sounded and, above all, do not point a loaded bow at anyone.

When in groups, archers should practice only if supervision is provided.

Once target assignments are made it is wise to shoot only at your own target.

Always be on the alert for clearance in back of your target. Someone might unintentionally cross the path of your arrow. All access points to the range should be fenced off to exclude pedestrians, but since this is not always possible, it is the archer's responsibility to be aware.

Etiquette in archery is a form of safety. Making loud noise when someone is shooting is rude and unsafe. A good archer feels a responsibility for everyone's safety and pleasure in shooting.

After an end of shooting it is recommended that you step back off the line. This will allow the field captain to call the signals safely and wisely.

At no time after the "shoot" signal is the area safe in front of the shooting line. Do not cross the line to see where your arrow landed or to retrieve a fallen arrow. No reason is valid enough to risk your safety.

Proper shooting clothing is essential. Avoid loose garments that will catch the string as well as necklaces, pendants, pins, pencils in pockets, bracelets, and buttons.

Arrows should be removed from the target in a manner that is safe to all archers on the target. Place one hand on the target while the other hand holds the arrow close to the point of entry and twists the arrow free. Pulling arrows can be dangerous. If one becomes imbedded and its removal is sudden while someone is standing in front of the target, there can be injury. It is recommended that the archer who is removing arrows stand to the side of the target to avoid hitting himself with the end of the arrow as it is removed.

As a rule, it is wise to follow the grain of the feather when removing a partially hidden arrow. If the feathers are hidden, either in turf or hay, pull the arrow through by the tip. This method protects the shaft and prolongs the life of the feathers.

Shooting aimlessly into the air is most dangerous. You can never be sure where the arrow will land. An archery range is not a place for fooling. It is both unsafe and discourteous to run, shout, or make loud noises. Consideration of others is one of the necessities in range procedure.

TECHNIQUE SAFETY

Keep the bow elbow rotated away from the string to avoid elbow bruises. The bow shoulder should be kept down and back when drawing a bow in order to avoid a shoulder bruise caused by a string slap on the release.

The armguard and finger tab should always be worn for protection. New archers might have sensitive fingers and it is recommended that they use Tincture of Benzoin, a skin toughener. Soreness of the fingers is caused by pinching the arrow or by a lazy third finger.

In order to protect the bowhand one should always use an arrow rest on the bow. When drawing the arrow, keep the forefinger of the bowhand around the grip of the bow. Many beginners place the forefinger around the arrow, which can be most dangerous if the arrow is accidentally released.

When a string slap occurs on the nose it is an indication that the archer's head is cocked to one side instead of facing the target.

Female archers are cautioned to keep the string close to the armpit on the outside of the chest.

String slap on the forearm or wrist is caused by moving these parts toward the string on the release. A correct grip will help the archer to avoid these injuries. An understrung bow (too-narrow string height) will cause wrist slaps.

6

Competition in Archery

From local fun shoots to international championship tournaments, archery competition is widespread, varied in nature, and always a stimulating activity for the participant. The archery range, with colorful windflags and long lines of archers in their traditional white uniforms, makes an impressive sight. The usual outfit for male archers consists of a pair of white long trousers and a white T-shirt; for women, a white skirt, long slacks, or shorts, and a white tailored blouse. The wearing of white when participating in a target archery tournament is an unwritten rule of conduct. An experienced archer is aware of the *code of conduct* used in tournaments, but since this code hasn't been printed for the novice, some of it will be included in this chapter.

The general demeanor of an archer can be included in a discussion of sportsmanship in archery, because behavior and conduct are based on the need to create a shooting environment which is conducive to good performance. An archer must concentrate in order to perform well, therefore quiet must prevail on the range during shooting. An archer expresses his good sportsmanship through courtesy to other archers. His speaking voice is low and he does nothing to distract the archer on the line. Temper outbursts are considered a distraction to other archers and are not condoned. Good sportsmanship means honesty in calling and recording scores as well as cooperation with officials and target mates. The archer should follow the tournament directions as given by the officials, and he should avoid fault-finding in situations as they arise. The code of conduct requires an archer to abide by the rules and accept the decisions of the officials in good spirit. A sense of fair play and honor are a part of good sportsmanship. An archer should be willing to share with other archers the advantages he wishes for himself; he should show a genuine interest in the problems of others and appreciation for their high performance. An honorable archer is one who has pride in himself as an archer and is respectful of the traditions of the sport he has chosen.

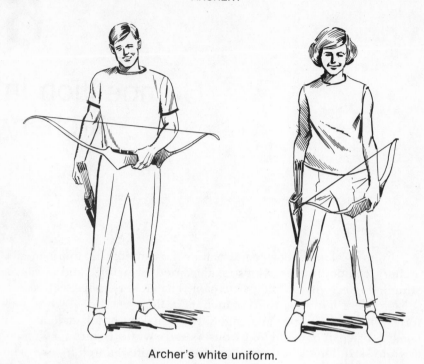

Archer's white uniform.

SIMPLIFIED RULES OF SHOOTING— NATIONAL ARCHERY ASSOCIATION

Tournament Conduct

The officials in an archery tournament are the Field Captain on the men's field and the Lady Paramount on the women's field. Archers must shoot and retrieve arrows in accordance with the whistle signals of the field official. The official is in charge of the tournament and all decisions made by that official are final. The main responsibilities of archery officials are to approve field conditions, enforce safety procedures, maintain order on the shooting line, conduct a legal tournament (all rules observed), penalize unsportsmanlike conduct, and make any decisions necessary at the targets.

Any archer who acts in an unsportsmanlike manner is removed from the tournament after receiving one warning from the field official.

Any kind of bow can be used, except a crossbow, compound bow, or any bow which would give undue advantage over other contestants. A bowsight that is not prismatic may be used. If any tackle breaks during the act of shooting, the arrow is considered shot. If an arrow falls from the bow as it is shot (mis-nock), it counts zero unless it can be reached with the bow. The archer is not allowed to cross the line to retrieve the fallen arrow.

Any kind of arrow is permitted except those that would cause unreasonable damage to the targets. Any type of release is permitted except one that is mechanical. Spotting aids and quivers may be used on the shooting line but must be removed when the archer steps off the line.

The archer should stand with a foot on either side of the shooting line. After completing his arrows, he should step back off the line at least three feet.

To shoot a round means to shoot a given number of ends from a given distance. When more than one distance is used, each distance in the round is called a range. No practice is allowed between various ranges when shooting in a tournament. The longest range is always shot first, then the next longest distance, and so forth until the round is completed. If an arrow hangs down across the face of the target the official will stop the shooting while he inserts the arrow correctly.

Any archer has the privilege of reporting unsafe conditions or unsportsmanlike conduct to the officials. A rule of courtesy states that an archer should remain on the shooting line until his target partner is finished shooting.

In all official competition, ends should be shot "three and three." Half of the archers assigned to the target shoot their first three arrows and step off the line. The other half come to the line to shoot their first three arrows and then they step off the line. The first group return to shoot their last three arrows, then the second group shoot their last three arrows. An archer is allowed 2½ minutes to shoot three arrows.

Scoring and Recording

An end consists of six arrows. Only six arrows can be shot at any one time. If more are shot, only the lowest six count. Arrows which hit the wrong target do not count for score.

The target face has five concentric circles and the most widely used face is 48 inches in diameter. The center circle (gold) counts nine points; the red counts seven points; the blue counts five points; the black counts three points; the white counts one point. The target petticoat (outside the white ring) counts zero. An arrow that cuts the line between two colors is given the higher value. An arrow that rebounds after hitting the scoring surface, if witnessed, counts seven

Target face value.

points. An arrow that passes through the scoring face, if witnessed, counts seven points.

An arrow must be left in the target until it has been recorded. If an arrow is imbedded in another arrow in the target, it counts the same score as the arrow into which it became imbedded. The end score is recorded from highest arrow value (9) to lowest (0). Example of an end score: 9, 9, 9, 7, 5, 3. A perfect end is one in which all six arrows are in the gold (54 points).

Ties are resolved in favor of the archer who has the greatest number of hits. If the score is still tied, the archer with the greatest number of golds (inner circle 10's) is the winner. If still tied, the archer with the greatest number of 9's is the winner. If still tied, both are declared equal.

If a target falls during an end, that end is shot over by all the archers on that target. If the value of an arrow is doubtful or if a perfect end has been shot, the field official should be called over before the target, face, or any arrow has been touched by anyone. He then decides the score of the doubtful arrow or witnesses the perfect end. If the target has been touched, the score value of the arrow is the lower of the two.

Each archer is responsible for seeing that his arrows are called correctly, recorded properly, and turned into the officials at the end of the round. Ten ring scoring, which is done in the F.I.T.A., 900, and 600 rounds, is done as follows: inner gold, ten points; outer gold, nine points; inner red, eight points; outer red, seven points; inner blue, six points; outer blue, five points; inner black, four points; outer black, three points; inner white, two points; outer white, one point.

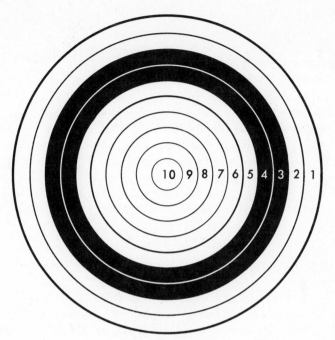

Ten ring scoring.

Double scoring.

The double scoring system is the official scorekeeping method which must be used in tournament shooting. Each archer on each target is given an assignment or duty according to position. The target assignment will list A, B, C, D, and the archer's name by one of these letters. Position A is the target captain, whose responsibility it is to call the value of every arrow on his target and to withdraw the arrows from the target. Positions B and C are scorekeepers. Each has a set of scoresheets, and each one independently records the value of the arrows as the target captain calls them out. These scorekeepers should check with each other after each end to compare scores and totals. If an error is discovered and the arrows are already out of the target, the lower of the two scores is considered official. Position D is the arrow retriever, who finds arrows that missed or passed through the target.

ARCHERY ROUNDS

An archery round is a standardized unit of competition with a prescribed number of arrows to be shot at a prescribed distance or distances. There are rounds to suit all levels of ability: championship and non-championship classes; men, women, and junior categories; and new and ancient rounds that vary target size and scoring method.

Championship Rounds

The Easton 600 Round   **48″**
(ten ring scoring)
20 arrows at 60 yards
20 arrows at 50 yards
20 arrows at 40 yards

The 900 Round   **48″**
(ten ring scoring)
30 arrows at 60 yards
30 arrows at 50 yards
30 arrows at 40 yards

The Men's F.I.T.A. Round
(ten ring scoring)
36 arrows at 90 meters   **122 cm.**
36 arrows at 70 meters   **122 cm.**
36 arrows at 50 meters   **80 cm.**
36 arrows at 30 meters   **80 cm.**

The Women's F.I.T.A. Round
(ten ring scoring)
36 arrows at 70 meters   **122 cm.**
36 arrows at 60 meters   **122 cm.**
36 arrows at 50 meters   **80 cm.**
36 arrows at 30 meters   **80 cm.**

Collegiate 600 Round   **48″**
(ten ring scoring)
20 arrows at 50 yards
20 arrows at 40 yards
20 arrows at 30 yards

Indoor F.I.T.A. Round   **40 cm.**
(ten ring scoring)
30 arrows at 18 meters

Non-Championship and Historical Rounds

The Columbia Round   **48″**
24 arrows at 50 yards
24 arrows at 40 yards
24 arrows at 30 yards

The Hereford Round   **48″**
72 arrows at 80 yards
48 arrows at 60 yards
24 arrows at 50 yards

Non-Championship and Historical Rounds (*Continued*)

The Junior American Round   48″
30 arrows at 50 yards
30 arrows at 40 yards
30 arrows at 30 yards

The St. George Round   48″
36 arrows at 100 yards
36 arrows at 80 yards
36 arrows at 60 yards

The Windsor Round   48″
36 arrows at 60 yards
36 arrows at 50 yards
36 arrows at 40 yards

The National Round   48″
48 arrows at 60 yards
24 arrows at 50 yards

The St. Nicholas Round   48″
48 arrows at 40 yards
36 arrows at 30 yards

The Team Rounds   48″
96 arrows at 60 yards — Men
96 arrows at 50 yards — Women

The Duryee Round   80 cm.
(ten ring scoring)
90 arrows at 30 yards

The 300 Indoor Round   16″
(5 arrows an end, scored 5-4-3-2-1)
black and white face
60 arrows at 20 yards

The Junior Columbia Round   48″
24 arrows at 40 yards
24 arrows at 30 yards
24 arrows at 20 yards

The American Round   48″
30 arrows at 60 yards
30 arrows at 50 yards
30 arrows at 40 yards

The Scholastic Round   48″
24 arrows at 40 yards
24 arrows at 30 yards

The Western Round   48″
48 arrows at 60 yards
48 arrows at 50 yards

The Clout Rounds   48″
36 arrows at 180 yards — Men
36 arrows at 140 yards — Women

The York Round   48″
72 arrows at 100 yards
48 arrows at 80 yards
24 arrows at 60 yards

The Chicago Round   16″
96 arrows at 20 yards

The 300 Outdoor Round   48″
(scored 5-4-3-2-1)
20 arrows at 60 yards
20 arrows at 50 yards
20 arrows at 40 yards

The P.A.A. Outdoor Round
(The P.A.A. Round is 20 targets, consisting of two 10-target segments. Each of ten targets is at a different distance. Each has a walk-up with three shooting positions and each position is at a different distance. One arrow is shot from each position. Scoring: 5-4-3.)

No. 1   16-18-20 yards at 14″ face
No. 2   21-23-25 yards at 14″ face
No. 3   24-27-30 yards at 14″ face
No. 4   29-32-35 yards at 22″ face
No. 5   34-37-40 yards at 22″ face
No. 6   39-42-45 yards at 22″ face
No. 7   43-46-50 yards at 22″ face
No. 8   47-51-55 yards at 30″ face
No. 9   52-56-60 yards at 30″ face
No. 10 57-61-65 yards at 30″ face

The P.A.A. Indoor Round   16″
Scoring as 300 Indoor Round
60 arrows at 20 yards

SCHOLASTIC ROUND

Name
Class

40 yards			Hits	Score
Distance score				
30 yards				
Distance score				
Total score				

COLUMBIA ROUND

Name
Class

50 yards			Hits	Score
Distance score				
40 yards				
Distance score				
30 yards				
Distance score				
Total score				

900 ROUND

Name
Class

50 yards			Hits	Score
Distance score				
40 yards				
Distance score				
30 yards				
Distance score				
Total score				

Scorecards.

Method of determining a custom-made round for archery classes

  1. level of shooting ability —————————————————————————.
  2. farthest distance available —————————————————————————.
  3. Time allotted for shooting —————————————————————————.
       (five to seven minutes needed per end)

Using these facts, make out a scorecard which could be used as your school round.

Round I

Name
Class

Round II

Name
Class

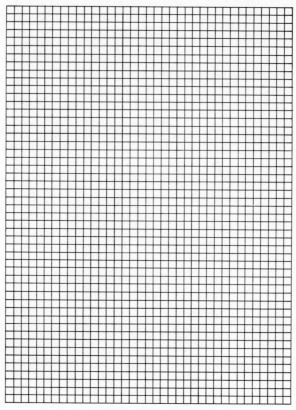

Daily score graph.

HANDICAP SCORES

A handicap system is used in some competitive events in which all participants begin on par with each other. Each archer is given a handicap score at the start of competition which has been determined by the average score of three rounds shot prior to the actual tournament. The formula for determining handicap score is as follows: Perfect score minus archer's average score = subtotal; 80 per cent of subtotal = handicap score.

Example for Columbia Round:

Perfect score	648
Archer's average	− 494
Subtotal	154
80% of Subtotal	× .80
	123.20
Handicap score	123 points

Work out your handicap score for a class round of five ends at 30 yards.

GUIDELINES FOR ADMINISTERING AN ARCHERY TOURNAMENT

An archery tournament can be an intramural event of one hour duration or a national event for four days duration. For any type of tournament certain basic needs are in common: targets, target stands, faces, scorecards, pencils, awards. As the level and prestige of a tournament rises the needs become more complex. Additional needs are: entry fees, amateur affidavits, name tags, refreshments, signs, scoreboards, and so forth. In the following organizational breakdown, the event in mind is one in which several schools would be entered for local or district competition.

Eight weeks prior to tournament, complete tournament information. To each school send the following: tournament date, place, name of director, address, and phone number; schedule of events, rounds to be shot, and time schedule; map and directions for archery range and school; lodging and eating facilities available, if needed; amateur regulations and affidavits; type of awards; and number of entries allowed, entry fees, and entry form.

Duties	Equipment Needed
Registration Committee	
Check amateur affidavits as they arrive.	One manila envelope for each entree.
Make out starting target assignments.	Name tags
Fill registration envelopes for each entree.	Programs
Distribute registration envelopes as archers arrive.	Starting target assignments
Awards Committee	
Purchase awards needed for tournament.	Trophies, medals, ribbons, as determined by the awards committee and financial condition.
Arrange a display during the duration of the tournament.	
Plan for the awards presentation.	
Range Committee	
Make a detailed layout of the field.	Targets, target faces, and nails.
Set up the field for shooting.	Windflags, bow racks or poles, benches and chairs, line marker, yard line signs, posts and ropes, any signs needed, and target numbers.
Replace target faces as needed.	
Reinforce targets as needed.	
Move field forward as rounds progress.	
Retrieve arrows which archers cannot find.	
Police the range, keep spectators behind ropes, etc.	

Duties	Equipment Needed

Scoring Committee

Plan the scoresheet.
Prepare scoresheets on clipboards
After each round collect scoresheets, re-assign archers to targets according to total score.
Redistribute clipboards for next round.
Help head scorer in determining the winners.
Prepare final results for printing and mailing to contestants.

Two clipboards and pencils for each target with scoresheets.
Master scoreboard or blackboard.
Felt pens.

Refreshments Committee

Plan refreshments and serve them.
Drinking water should be available to archers.

Refreshment table and utensils for service.
Waste cans.

Official's Assistants

Control the signs indicating which archers should be on the line first.
Stay with official to perform necessary tasks such as timing archers when requested to do so.

Indicator signs for archers, stopwatch, field horn, and chair for official.
Emergency field box that contains tape, scissors, pins, extra pencils, bandages, etc.

GENERAL RECOMMENDATIONS

Officials needed are a field captain or lady paramount as the head official, assistants as needed, and a head scorer. Rules of shooting should be those of the National Archery Association. A copy of these rules can be obtained from Mr. Clayton Shenk, Lancaster, Pennsylvania 17601.

In order to determine the entry fee the following steps are suggested: Make a list of all the items you will need in order to run the tournament. Use the suggested "Equipment Needed" under committee organization, and your own committee suggestions. Determine which of these items will be furnished by your school, contributed by local archers or clubs, or donated by sporting goods companies. Establish the cost of the remaining items which will be purchased, and divide that cost by the number of archers you estimate will enter the tournament.

The first tournament will cost more than the subsequent ones, therefore the entry fee for the first tournament should be slightly higher than the anticipated cost. Any funds left over could be contributed to the second meet. Remember, it is always easier to lower the fee than to raise it.

The first tournament should be kept as simple as possible and need not be any longer than it takes to shoot one round. Awards can be homemade if money is not available for trophies or medals. Examples: use arrows sprayed gold, with lettering (1st place); use masonite and paint to make arrowhead-shaped plaques with targets painted on, or the last six inches of the feathered end of the arrow sprayed and glued on; use the traditional archery tassel made of yarn.

Amateur Affidavit

Gentlemen: "In accordance with the Amateur Rules of The National Archery Association, I herewith state and affirm that I have read and understood the rules of The National Archery Association of the United States and that I am an amateur according to those rules."

Signature of archer   Address

NATIONAL ARCHERY ASSOCIATION
of the UNITED STATES
RULES and REGULATIONS
GOVERNING AMATEUR COMPETITION

1. *PRIZES* — The amateur archer shall not compete for cash. Awards shall not exceed the cost of $70.00 for first place, $40.00 for second place, and $30.00 for third place. Challenge trophies and other similar prizes may be authorized by the Eligibility Committee and approved by the National Archery Association Board of Governors.

2. *EXHIBITIONS* — The amateur archer shall not exhibit his skill as an archer for personal monetary gain.

3. *INSTRUCTION* — The amateur archer shall not accept pay for coaching. A school or college teacher (including physical education teachers) and other individuals such as camp counselors and those working for community organizations, recreation associations or councils, or religious, eleemosynary organizations, or other non-profit entities whose work is solely educational and who are not paid for coaching for competition shall be eligible as amateurs.

4. *ENDORSEMENT* — The amateur shall not permit his name or picture to be used in print, over television, radio, or other public communication system, in an advertisement or in the endorsement of any company or product. The use of an archer's photograph in news media or the participation in radio broadcast or telecast is not prohibited, provided the archer receives no compensation of any kind, directly or indirectly, in connection with the use of such photograph or such participation provided permission is granted by the Eligibility Committee.

5. *EXPENSES* — The maximum expenses which an amateur archer may request, receive, or accept in connection with his competition or participation in any event, exhibition, or tournament, shall not exceed (a) his actual expenditures for travel up to the cost of first class public transportation fare, including the cost

of such transportation to and from airport or railroad terminal; and (b) his actual expenditures for maintenance, including lodging, and meals, up to a total of twenty ($20) dollars per day for each day during the time occupied between going to and returning from the event, exclusive of necessary travel time. The period for which expenses may be allowed shall not exceed one (1) day after the event unless for good reason a longer period is expressly approved by the National Archery Association Board of Governors; (c) vouchers or receipts evidencing payment of actual expenditures for transportation and lodging shall be furnished by the archer and attached to the expense statement to be submitted to the National Archery Association Board of Governors. If in any case an archer has been unable to obtain reasonably suitable hotel accommodations and/or meals at a cost within the amount allowable above, and if in any one or more days he has been required to spend more than such allowable amount, the sponsoring organization and the archer may jointly apply to the National Archery Association Board of Governors for permission to pay and accept respectively a supplemental allowance for expenses equal to the excess amount the archer has been required to spend in any such day or days, but which supplemental allowance shall in no event exceed five ($5) dollars for any one day.

6. *EMPLOYMENT BY A FIRM* — The amateur archer shall not accept money from a firm or individual engaged in some phase of archery promotion without regularly being on the payroll and working at a specific job in that organization. If he is employed by an archery manufacturer or sales firm, he shall not receive paid time off during the normal work week (35 hours) for the practice of archery and shall not have his expenses paid in any way by the firm in which he is employed. The above shall not preclude attending a tournament during the normal two-week paid vacation period available to most people.

7. *SELF-EMPLOYMENT* — The amateur archer if self-employed in the manufacture of archery tackle must not use his shooting prowess or his name or photograph as a basis for selling his wares.

8. *AMATEUR COMPETITION WITH A PROFESSIONAL* — The amateur may participate for awards or prizes in open competition with the professional in competitive events below the State level where the prizes or awards do not violate rule #1 of these amateur regulations. The professional may participate with the amateur in State, Regional, National or International events but shall not compete for the same titles, prizes, or awards as the amateur. Open events or tournaments, exhibitions or clinics shall be registered and sanctioned by the National Archery Association in advance of such events.

9. *REINSTATEMENT TO ELIGIBILITY TO COMPETE AS AN AMATEUR* — Any archer professionalized under these regulations, regardless of age, may apply for reinstatement to amateur status, and if such application is approved, be eligible to participate in amateur competition *after one year* from the date of last acts of professionalism. An archer shall be reinstated only upon recommendation of the Eligibility Committee and approval of the National Archery Association Board of Governors. An archer so

reinstated shall not be eligible to compete in any State Championships, District (2 or more states) Championship, National Championship, International competition or Olympic Games.

10. *EFFECTIVE DATE* — The effective date of these regulations is September 1, 1965.

ORGANIZATIONS

The following list represents the archery organizations that foster the growth of archery as a sport through tournament sponsorship and control of the rules of shooting, classification of archers, amateur status, equipment advancement, teacher training schools, and publicity.

NATIONAL ARCHERY ASSOCIATION (NAA). 1951 Geraldson Drive, Lancaster, Pennsylvania 17601. The NAA represents the sport of archery on the U. S. Olympic committee; governs amateur regulations; governs the rules of target archery; sponsors a national championship and chooses and sponsors teams to represent the U.S. in World Championship tournaments for Target and Field Archery.

NATIONAL FIELD ARCHERY ASSOCIATION (NFAA). Rt. 2, Box 514, Redlands, California 92373. The NFAA governs the rules of field archery competition in the United States; classification of field archers (barebow, free-style); sponsors a national championship.

AMERICAN INDOOR ARCHERY ASSOCIATION (AIAA). P.O. Box 174, Grayling, Michigan 49738. The AIAA governs the rules of indoor archery as used in indoor lanes in the United States.

PROFESSIONAL ARCHERS ASSOCIATION (PAA). Rt. 1, Box 32, Hickory Corners, Michigan 49060. The PAA is an organization devoted to the promotion of tournaments which have large monetary prizes; promotion of professionalism in archery; instructor courses; rules and regulations which govern the professional archer.

ARCHERY MANUFACTURERS ORGANIZATION (AMO). R.D. #1, Box 119, Bechtelsville, Pennsylvania 19505. The AMO is an organization which advances the sale of archery equipment through projects in archery education, standardization of equipment, and sponsorship of archery events.

7

Testing Devices in Archery

Testing devices are varied in archery, from a rating form which lists all the segments of shooting technique to the scorecard used during each shooting session. In archery, a student has a daily evaluation of his efforts and skill through his scorecard. The higher the skill level, the higher the score. Rarely heard from an archery student is the question, "How am I doing?" The archer knows *how* he is doing with every arrow he releases; more often he does not know *what* he is doing. The rating form and arrow chart are two main ways of testing the technique of the archery student and evaluating the degree of consistency that he has attained.

THE ARROW CHART

The arrow chart is a method used for evaluating shooting technique by either teacher or student. It is a method based on the premise that, if shooting technique and equipment are perfect, every arrow will land dead center in the target; if the technique is not perfect the arrows will be scattered or grouped in another part of the target. Every fault in shooting technique causes the arrow to fly in a particular direction away from the center.

Through the efforts of coaches and archers in past experiments a list of causes and effects are available which tells us the faults of shooting and the corresponding flight direction. For example, if a right-handed archer uses his left eye for aiming instead of his right, all his arrows will group to the left of the target; if an archer moves his head or bow on the release to "peek" after his arrow, his grouping will be high and to the right of the target center. An archer can partially compensate for faulty technique by adjusting his bowsight, but compensation in aiming will not wholly eradicate the faulty arrow flight.

The specific function of the arrow chart, which is a picture of a

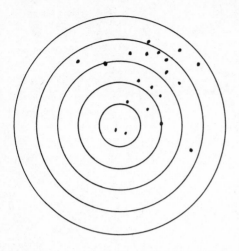

Sample arrow chart.

target, is to allow the archer to plot the position of each arrow that he shoots and, hopefully, to determine his grouping. After many arrows have been shot and their positions recorded, grouping is shown on paper. Knowing the arrow grouping is a valuable asset to both the archer and his teacher. The cause and effect list included in this chapter should be consulted and, by the process of elimination, the archer can discover and eliminate his major faults in shooting technique.

For a successful arrow chart the following rules are suggested: Allow yourself one practice end for initial bowsight adjustment. After you start to plot arrow positions make any bowsight adjustment you

Arrow chart.

Name _____   Grouping _____

Class_____   Technique fault_____

Arrow chart.

deem necessary. By doing this, you will eliminate the reason for an undesirable grouping if your sight setting was wrong. Shoot at least 30 arrows, preferably 40 to 50. Make use of a very small, very dark dot as the arrow symbol. This is particularly essential for the more advanced archer who is capable of shooting tighter groupings close to the center of the target.

In most instances the grouping is evident, but if you wish, you may divide the target into four equal parts and count the arrows in each section. Then refer to the following lists of reasons why arrows group in certain ways. Try a little self-analysis, and then ask someone to watch you shoot. The following lists refer to faults committed by right-handed archers; reverse for left-handed archers.

REASONS FOR ARROWS GROUPING LEFT

Fault	Correction
1. Hunched bow shoulder.	1. Squeeze shoulder blades together on the draw. Pull more, push less.
2. Gripping the bow too tightly.	2. Hold loosely. Use a sling of some sort which will provide security.
3. Flinching the bow arm.	3. Check the position of the bow elbow as part of your check list to assure you that it will not be hit by the string.
4. Hitting arm, wrist, clothing. (Low and left)	4. Tighten or remove bulky clothing. Use a shirt protector and armguard. Keep your arm still on the release.
5. String catching on finger-tab.	5. Use a new tab if the leather is curling tightly.
6. Tilting top of bow to the left.	6. Check for even distribution of weight on the feet; use a level; keep string alignment steady.
7. Pinching the arrow nock.	7. Separate your fingers slightly on the string.
8. Pulling with hand muscles. (cupped hand)	8. Keep the back of the hand straight across the knuckles; pull with your back muscle.
9. Stiffening the bow arm on the release.	9. Concentrate and try to be more relaxed.
10. Using the left eye for aiming.	10. Close or cover the left eye until you can control the aiming eye.
11. Weight on the heels. (leaning back)	11. Be aware of weight distribution at the start of each shot.
12. Body aligned to left side of target.	12. Keep feet, hips, and shoulders on the target line.
13. Twisting bow wrist on release.	13. Check for correct grip position; wear a wrist support.
14. Arrow shaft away from the bow on release.	14. Control finger motion and tension while in the anchor position.
15. Incorrect bowsight setting; overspined arrows.	15. Move sight to the left, change to weaker arrows.
16. String alignment too far to the right of the bow.	16. Check string position at chin and nose; move string into center of bow.
17. Release hand moving outward away from face.	17. Keep release hand fingers touching neck or jawbone.

REASONS FOR ARROWS GROUPING RIGHT

Fault	Correction
1. Moving bow to the right on release.	1. Set bow shoulder firmly; aim into the release as long as possible.
2. Bow tilting to the right.	2. Check weight distribution on feet; use a level; keep string alignment steady.
3. Holding string too deeply in fingers.	3. Place string in first joints only.
4. Release hand moving inward to neck.	4. Relax the fingers; stay directly behind the arrow nock.
5. String alignment too far left of the bow.	5. Check string position at chin and nose; move string toward center of bow.
6. Twisting bow wrist on release.	6. Check for correct grip position and wear a wrist support.
7. Peeking.	7. Aim longer into the release; keep head and bow still; practice opening the left eye after the release.
8. Outwardly bent wrist. (string hand)	8. Straighten wrist into line with knuckles and elbow.
9. Incorrect bowsight setting; arrows underspined; feathers too large.	9. Move sight to the right; use heavier arrows; use smaller feathers.

REASONS FOR ARROWS GROUPING HIGH

Fault	Correction
1. Arrow nocked too low.	1. Relocate proper nocking position.
2. Bow arm raised on the release.	2. Keep bow hand in line with the gold; aim as long into the release as possible; check for sight in or near gold during the follow through.
3. Lazy third finger.	3. Keep equal pressure on all fingers of the string hand.
4. Heeling the bow.	4. Keep bow hand pressure off the heel of the hand; transfer pressure toward the upper center part of the hand.
5. Anchoring while mouth is open.	5. Clench your teeth.
6. Using raised forefinger of the bowhand as shelf.	6. Keep the fingers of the bowhand in the grip section of the bow.
7. Drawing beyond anchor position.	7. Maintain three-point contact of your nose, chin, and jaw.
8. Drawing more arrow than usual.	8. Use draw check method to determine amount of arrow drawn each time.
9. Release hand snapping down toward chest.	9. Try to feel your release hand stay along neck; relax hand and fingers when releasing.
10. Anchoring below normal position.	10. Feel the string hand firmly against the underside of the jawbone.
11. Leaning away from the target.	11. Equalize weight on both feet.
12. Holding the bow grip too low.	12. Hold in the center of the grip for proper balance.
13. Inhaling just before the release which raises the shoulders.	13. Air should be exhaled before serious aiming, and a static position held until arrow is released.

REASONS FOR ARROWS GROUPING LOW

Fault	Correction
1. Incomplete draw.	1. Feel all contact points of the anchor position; use draw check method.
2. Creeping.	2. Maintain the secondary draw; tighten the muscles of upper back and arm.
3. Dropping the bow hand or arm on release.	3. Keep pointing arm at the gold. Keep aiming.
4. Head or chin reaching forward to meet string.	4. Maintain normal standing position; bring string to you; do not reach with your head.
5. Nocking arrow too high.	5. Relocate correct nocking position.
6. Dead release or forward moving.	6. Move hand back along neck for a dynamic or flying release.
7. Higher anchor than usual.	7. Index finger shelf of the right hand should be firmly under jawbone.
8. Leaning toward target.	8. Equalize weight on both feet and keep it there.
9. Collapsing the bow arm.	9. Lock shoulder in the pre-draw; maintain arm level; point arm into gold.
10. Exhaling on the release.	10. Exhale before aiming begins.
11. Aiming below the gold.	11. Do not release until the bowsight is in the center of the gold.
12. Webbing the bow.	12. Keep your hand in contact with the grip of the bow and exert pressure closer to the center of the hand.
13. Pulling bow with the forearm (right elbow close to chest).	13. The right arm should look like an extension of the arrow.

REASONS FOR A LATERAL DISPERSION

Fault	Correction
1. A floating or inconsistent string alignment.	1. Establish a definite string position and maintain it until the arrow is released.
2. Inconsistencies in the hands. (bow and string)	2. Check lists for left and right groupings which deal with release hand and bow hand.
3. Any combination of faults listed for arrows going left and right.	3. A complete analysis of your shooting technique is needed. Ask for help.

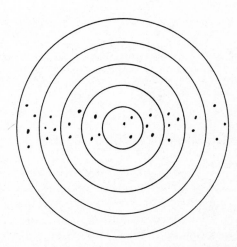

Lateral dispersion.

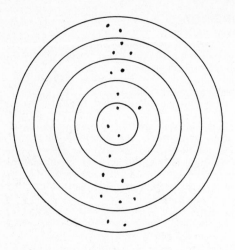

Vertical dispersion.

REASONS FOR VERTICAL DISPERSION

Fault	Correction
1. Inconsistent nocking point.	1. Mark and use your nocking point.
2. Lack of consistent amount of draw.	2. Use a draw check method.
3. Poor secondary draw.	3. Draw, hold, and release the same amount of energy for each arrow shot.
4. Inconsistencies in the arms. (bow and string)	4. Check lists for high and low groupings which deal with the bow arm and string arm.

REASONS FOR SCATTERED PATTERNS

Fault	Correction
1. A bow too heavy to control.	1. Change to a lighter weight bow.
2. Arrows too long. (inability to determine draw check)	2. Change to arrows of the correct length.
3. Inaccuracies in aiming.	3. Release only when sight is steady in the middle of the gold.
4. Physical weakness. (inability to hold and aim the lightest bow)	4. A program of body building would be in order for this deficiency.
5. A combination of faults.	5. A complete analysis of your technique is needed. Follow the advice of your teacher or coach.
6. Snap shooting.	6. Slow down!

COMPARATIVE SCORES

In comparing his scores to a standard achievement chart or to actual score records established by other archers, an archery student finds his own comparative level of achievement, and can then set a realistic goal for future performances. Both types of comparison scores are included here. The collegiate all-time archery records were com-

ARCHERY TECHNIQUE RATING FORM

Name ——————— Class ——————— Grade ———————

	SELF-EVALUATION	1	2	FINAL
STANCE				
Foot position — square or open				
Body position — square or open				
Head position — facing target squarely				
NOCK				
Cock feather up				
String in joints of fingers				
Nock perpendicular to arrow rest				
DRAW				
Proper hand and wrist position				
Relaxed bow hand				
Rotated bow elbow				
Low bow shoulder				
String touching Nose				
String touching Chin				
Firm anchor				
Flat drawing hand				
Third finger on string				
String arm elbow in line with arrow				
Body and bow alignment				
Avoidance of creeping				
AIM				
Held long enough to steady down				
Archer does not snap shoot				
RELEASE				
Bow arm held level				
Bow hand relaxed				
String hand moves backwards smoothly				
Bow arm avoids flinching				
Archer does not "peek"				
FOLLOW-THROUGH				
Position held				

puted from published results of on-the-line and postal meets in local, regional, and national competition in which collegiate archers participated.

COLLEGIATE ALL-TIME ARCHERY RECORDS (June 1975)

Easton 600 Round

Women:	1974	Carol Jurn, Arizona State University	548
	1974	Linda Wilson, San Bernardino Valley	540
	1975	Debbie Green, Riverside City College	535
Men:	1974	Kevin Erlandson, San Bernardino Valley	562
	1975	Don Rabska, San Bernardino Valley	560
	1974	Steven Lieberman, Arizona State University	559

900 Round

Women:	1974	Debbie Green, Riverside City College	828
	1974	Janet Kemmerer, East Stroudsburg State	820
	1974	Luann Ryon, Riverside City College	819
Men:	1971	Gale Cavallin, San Bernadino Valley	853
	1975	Don Rabska, San Bernardino Valley	848
	1974	Gary Riley, San Bernardino Valley	847

American Round

Women:	1973	Monica Estes, San Bernardino Valley	742
	1970	Rose Svarc, San Bernardino Valley	730
	1969	Susan Vancas, University of Arizona	724
Men:	1971	Gale Cavallin, San Bernardino Valley	796
	1974	Don Rabska, San Bernardino Valley	788
	1974	Rick Stonebraker, Penn State University	786

F.I.T.A. Round

Women:	1974	Luann Ryon, Riverside City College	1222
	1974	Debbie Green, Riverside City College	1219
	1974	Janice Smith, San Bernardino Valley	1171
Men:	1974	Steve Lieberman, Arizona State University	1255
	1974	Gary Riley, San Bernardino Valley	1218
	1975	Don Rabska, San Bernardino Valley	1216

THE COLLEGE ARCHERY DEVELOPMENT PROGRAM

Qualifying Distances for Outdoors

	A	AA	AAA	Champion
36 Arrows at 30 meters — 80 cm.	240	260	280	300
36 Arrows at 40 meters — 80 cm.	240	260	280	300
36 Arrows at 50 meters — 80 cm.	220	240	260	280
36 Arrows at 60 meters — 122 cm. — 48"	220	240	260	280
36 Arrows at 70 meters — 122 cm. — 48"	220	240	260	280
36 Arrows at 90 meters — 122 cm. — 48" (MEN Only)	200	220	240	260

Tournament Rounds

	A	AA	AAA	Champion
F.I.T.A. Round	900	950	1000	1050
900 Round	740	760	780	800

Qualifying Distances for Indoors

	A	AA	AAA	Champion
36 Arrows at 10 yards — 16" face	240	260	280	300
36 Arrows at 15 yards — 24" face	240	260	280	300
36 Arrows at 20 yards — 36" face	240	260	280	300
36 Arrows at 20 yards — 24" face	240	260	280	300
36 Arrows at 20 yards — 16" face	240	260	280	300

Tournament Round

	A	AA	AAA	Champion
Indoor F.I.T.A. — 18 m.	200	220	240	260

8

Archery Games

Archery games can be team or individual events, and take many forms. Some variations of archery have been mentioned in Chapter 1: bow hunting, bow fishing, flight, roving, clout, and archery golf. This section is designed to fit the needs of a school situation, with amount of space and large numbers of participants used as criteria for determining the games presented.

TEAM EVENTS

The following games are played by teams, and all follow the same basic organization. Each team is lined up as for a relay; each team has its own target; the number of archers on a team depends on the number of targets available and the number of archers in the group. Only the first person in the line is allowed to nock an arrow, and after shooting one arrow he moves to the end of the line. Each team should have a captain who keeps score and directs his team. The team having the greatest number of hits or points is declared the winner.

Tic-Tac-Toe

Equipment: Balloons; 15 yards range space.

Procedure: Nine balloons on each target are placed in three rows of three balloons each. First team to hit three balloons in any line is declared the winner.

Variation: At the end of the tic-tac-toe game, the remainder of the balloons can be shot in blackout competition (first team to break every balloon is the winner).

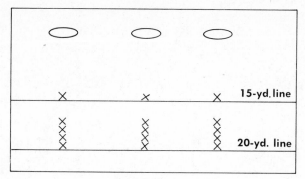

Team line-up.

Bird Shooting

Equipment: Flu flu arrows, 6 circular cardboard discs (12 to 16 inches); clear range space.

Procedure: The bird thrower tosses the circular disc up, across, and about 10 yards in front of the players, who are holding bows and nocked arrows. The next disc is thrown when the next players in line are ready. The team with the greatest number of hits within a certain time limit is declared the winner.

Variation: On a breezy day balloons can be released along the ground for "rabbit shooting." Same scoring as for bird shooting.

Wand Shooting

Equipment: One-inch strip of masking tape placed on the target face from top to bottom; 15 yards range space.

Procedure: One point for hitting the tape. Winner of the game is the team winning two out of three points.

Bingo

Equipment: Target face made to represent a Bingo card; 15 yards range space.

Procedure: First team to hit five squares in any line is the winner.

William Tell

Equipment: Target representing boy with an apple on his head; 15 yards range space.

Procedure: First team to hit the apple is the winner; any team member hitting the picture of the boy is eliminated.

INDIVIDUAL EVENTS

Flight Shooting

Equipment: 200 to 300 yards of clear, safe space; regular equipment.

Procedure: Flight shooting is won by the individual shooting an arrow the greatest distance. Success depends on the cast of the bow used. Holding the bow at a 45-degree angle will send an arrow the farthest distance a bow is capable of sending an arrow.

The Long Beach Work-Up

Equipment: Regular class issue, target faces, and distances.

Procedure: The purpose is to work up to target 1, where highest scorers in the class shoot. Start with three or four students on a target. After each end the highest scorer on the target moves up one while the lowest scorer on each target moves down one target.

Clout Shooting

Equipment: Stake (five-foot) in the center of the target with balloon or flag attached to the top; clout target marked on the ground in five concentric circles measuring 48 feet in diameter. The concentric circles are drawn in proportion to the standard target face (48 inches), a proportion of one foot to one inch. Shooting distance can vary from 80 yards to 120 yards depending on bow weight and experience of archer. Tournament distances for clout shooting are 120 and 140 yards for women; 180 yards for men.

Procedure: The entire group shoots at the same time; six arrows constitutes an end. If a light bow is used, the bowsight will need to be placed below the grip and sighted on the flag in the center of the target. A bow will deliver maximum distance when held at a 45-degree angle. Five scorekeepers are appointed, one to each color band, to remove all arrows in their respective areas. The arrows are collected, sorted according to length and crest, and placed side by side in the color band from which they were removed. Each archer then comes into the target area singly when called by the official, and as they collect and call out the value of each arrow, the two recording score-

Clout shooting bow angle.

keepers write down the score. The score values on a clout target are the same as on a standard target face—gold, 9; red, 7; blue, 5; black, 3; white, 1—and are determined by the position of the arrow tip.

Variation: Instead of marking the target on the ground, a rope, loosely attached to the base of the stake, can be used for convenience, ease, and speed. The rope, which is 24 feet long, is marked off in 4.8-foot segments painted gold, red, blue, black, and white. The score-keepers line up on one side of the rope in back of their designated colors and pick up all arrows which touch their colors. A sixth person moves the rope once around the circumference of the circle. The remainder of the scoring procedure is the same as above.

Archery Golf

Equipment: Golf course; 9-inch cloth ball target by the side of each green.

Procedure: Shoot as many arrows down the fairway as needed to reach and hit the special target by the green. The archer who takes the least number of shots in reaching the objective is the winner. The rules of archery golf are similar to golf rules. The following list of

ARCHERY GOLF CARD

Holes	Yards	Par	Players									
1	215	3										
2	230	3										
3	110	2										
4	142	2										
5	100	2										
6	170	3										
	967	15										

rules are used at Teela-Wooket Archery Camp and are quoted here, since official rules do not exist.

1. Each group shall select a captain to make decisions and to record scores *after* leaving *each* green.

2. Only *one* bow may be used unless it is broken, in which case the shot may be taken over with another bow without penalty. The same applies to a broken bowstring.

3. Arrows of any kind may be used.

4. Each shot counts *one*; also, each penalty.

5. The stand for a field shot, which may be a flight or an approach shot, must be directly behind the point of landing of the previous shot.

6. The archer with the lowest score on each target shoots first.

7. After the tee shot, the archer farthest from the target shoots first. *Do not advance until the shot is completed.*

8. Full draw is not required. The bow may be held in any position.

9. An arrow in an unplayable position may be shot from a point at equal or greater distance from the target, with a penalty of one point added.

10. A lost arrow, if not found in five minutes, may be replaced by another which is shot from a spot agreed upon by the group, with a penalty of one point added.

11. A shot may be conceded, with one point added to the score, if an arrow lands near enough to the target so that the archer can make the point of his nocked arrow touch the target. The feet must remain in their stance behind the spot where the point of the previously shot arrow landed.

12. The target may be turned to face the archer shooting.

13. "Fast" is the term used if it is necessary to signal anyone on the course.

14. In case of a tie there shall be a play-off.

9

Skill Advancement Techniques

To advance in archery skills means to perform the basic techniques more precisely, accurately, and consistently. It also means being practiced enough to use different kinds of equipment and accessories with effectiveness. The methods for improving techniques and accessories which aid in the perfection of technique will be discussed jointly.

PERFECTING THE DRAW

GRIP AND HAND LOCATOR. The position of the bow hand in the grip will determine the bow position on the release; consequently it will have effect on the flight of the arrow. Sometimes an archer will experience difficulty in determining the exact location of the grip position each time he draws. If the grip changes, the arrow flight changes. To avoid an inconsistent flight pattern a set grip position is used. To help locate the same position each time an archer can use a homemade or a commercial hand locator. The commercial locator is a leather ridge attached to the grip section of the bow. The archer feels the ridge in the same spot of his hand every time he begins to draw. The homemade locator is a method of aligning two lines, one on the bow with one on the hand. A piece of tape ⅛ inch wide is placed on the grip on or near the pivot point; another piece of tape is placed on the hand so that the two tapes line up when the archer is in a good grip position. The size and shape of bow grips vary with manufacturers, and also within the line of bow designs of one manufacturer. An archer should choose, after trying many, a bow grip that suits his hand structure for comfort, balance, and control.

BODY CHECK. Just as every archer has check points on his face during the anchor position, some archers have a body check with the string as it is drawn to the chest area. Body structure and shooting style determine whether or not an archer will have a body check or

Shirt protector.

contact point on his body with the string. Most archers who do have a body check wear a shirt protector which is made of plastic or leather. The protector keeps the string from catching on the clothing (which sends arrows low and left on the target). If the archer does draw the string into his body he should use this contact point as a body check by always consciously touching in the same spot for each draw.

DRAW CHECK DEVICE.   This is any accessory which notifies the archer that his arrow has reached the full draw position. In learning to do a draw check the beginning archer does a visual check on the position of the tip of the arrow. If this method does not prove accurate enough or the archer has difficulty in performing the skill correctly because of body structure, he can resort to any commercial draw check device. The most popular is called a "clicker" and is based on an audio signal delivered when the arrow tip has reached its

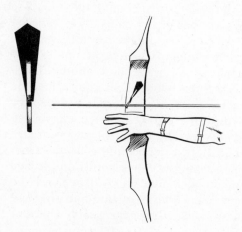

Clicker in use on the bow.

full draw position. The clicker is a metal strip attached to the side of the bow. The arrow is placed under the metal strip at the start of the draw. Throughout the primary draw the arrow moves back under the strip and when the tip of the arrow comes past the strip, the metal snaps down to make a clicking sound. The archer does not need to look at the tip of the arrow since he needs only to hear the sound to know he can release the arrow if it is properly aimed. Other commercially produced check devices are made of rubber tubing or flaps of material like plastic, which indicate by movement or sound that the arrow has reached its full draw position.

A draw check accessory is also of value if an archer is unable to complete a draw, or hold the draw during the aim, or aim where or as long as he wishes. Fear of failure, apprehension, or a habit which cannot be broken sometimes leads to psychological problems in shooting which seem insurmountable. If any problems arise involving the draw and aim the archer should try using a draw check device at least as long as it takes him to gain control of his shooting. An example of this extra use of a draw check device: As an archer brings his bowsight towards the gold to start the aiming he gets as far as the outside of the gold area and cannot move the sight into the gold. It seems to him that he is locked into immobility. His arm becomes immobile in the red or blue. This is a common phenomenon among archers and can be corrected most times by the draw check device. The archer must wait for the sound of the draw check device to permit his release and so before the sound he is "free" to move his sight wherever he wishes. The use of this device slows down shooting, giving the archer the advantage of control and analysis time. The device becomes a confidence builder and shares in the responsibility of triggering the release. It should be used until the archer can once more be master of his responses in the draw and aim.

PERFECTING THE ANCHOR

USE OF THE THUMB.   Using the thumb while anchoring is most often discouraged because it can do more damage than good—the thumb is a difficult appendage to control and use correctly. There is one exception, in which the use of the thumb should be tried in order to correct faults in the anchor position. In one theory of the anchor the thumb is used as a holding force and, as such, could conceivably be an advantage. It is worth a try for the archer who finds his anchor position slipping forward due to a poor secondary draw, or for the archer with a desire to release sooner than he knows he should. The right thumb leads back in an extended position and is hooked behind the neck, while the three middle fingers stay under the jawbone in the anchor position described in Chapter 3. The thumb is down and back as it hooks behind the neck and in this position holds the anchor in place, not allowing it to move forward. This holding force makes solid an otherwise floating anchor and narrows the vertical dispersion of arrows on the target.

KISS BUTTON.   This is a small plastic disk placed on the string so that it touches the lips of the archer in a full draw and anchor. The feel of the kiss button assures the archer that the anchor is at the same elevation on his jawbone. This accessory is used by those archers who have difficulty in finding the same, solid anchor on each draw. In order for the kiss button to be most effective, the teeth must be clenched, and the lips together in a normal state of relaxation. If the teeth are not clenched the jawbone will rise and fall and the kiss button will sit high or low on the lips. The result is a vertical dispersion of arrows on the target. If the lips reach out to meet the kiss button or string, the anchor position will not be solid, since the string will not be able to properly approach the face. This also will create a vertical dispersion of arrows, with most of them low on the target and a few as high as the gold.

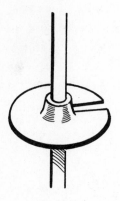

Kiss button.

PERFECTING THE AIM

The aiming period is a crucial time, requiring steadiness and stillness to pinpoint the bowsight in the exact middle of the gold. To breathe at such a time damages severely the quality of the aim. During the stance and nock segments of technique the archer should breathe deeply and heavily to build up an oxygen store. Just prior to aiming, the air in the lungs should be exhaled and in that static condition aiming should take place. Not until well into the follow-through should breathing resume. Intake of air raises the upper part of the body and output lowers it; either of these movements will have serious effect on aiming and arrow flight.

PERFECTING THE RELEASE

Many hours are devoted to the practice of the release, particularly for the release hand. The action of coming off the string must be smooth and perfectly timed if the release is to be considered good. The coordination between back muscle and right finger muscle action must be perfect. A good practice technique for the release hand takes place at five yards from the target with both eyes closed. The archer sets the bowsight very high on the sight bar, stands within five yards of the target, draws the arrow, anchors the string, and aims the sight in the gold. He then closes his eyes; remains stationary a few seconds, then releases the arrow while his eyes remain closed. When the eyes are closed the archer can concentrate completely on the release without interference from target, arrow, sight, or bow. Most archers are amazed at how clear the release action is when the eyes are closed, and find that corrections are easier to make. The release faults are very evident when the archer releases with his eyes closed. This practice technique is safe providing the archer performs the draw check and aim before he closes his eyes.

The bow wrist and hand should be relaxed during the release. It is essential that an archer use a finger sling or bow sling which allows him to relax his wrist and hand. The sling is the archer's guarantee that the bow will not fall to the ground. With this kind of security the archer is free to perform correctly. Try this experiment without equipment: Hold the bow arm in front of the body with a totally relaxed wrist. The left hand has to be drooping if the wrist is relaxed. If the hand is up and the wrist is cocked it indicates muscle tension. *Relax.* With the right hand hooked into the web of the left hand, pull back. You will note that the left wrist is now in a cocked position, not through its own efforts but forced by the pull of the right hand. This pull of the right hand is comparable to the bow pressure as exerted on the left hand in the draw. Now, let go with the right hand. If the left hand falls into its original drooping position, it indicates a relaxed left wrist. If the left wrist remains cocked it indicates tension. *Relax.* Study the accompanying diagrams which show the bow wrist and bow hand action on the draw and release.

A major fault during or immediately following the release is peeking. This is the action of moving the head to the left to watch the arrow hit, and at the same time moving the bow out of the way to the right. Peeking causes arrows to go high and to the right of the target. Beginners are obvious in their peeking action and can actually send the arrow off the target high on the right side; advanced archers have better control and are more subtle in the peeking action. Their arrows will group at one o'clock or two o'clock in the red or blue. Peeking is a fault which is difficult to correct because it is so natural for an archer to want to know where his arrows are going. It is not the fact of seeing the arrows land that is bad about peeking, but rather the head and bow movement which throws the arrow high and right. If by mental concentration the archer cannot control his physical reactions, the following two remedies are suggested for correcting peeking.

1. As the arrow is released, open the left eye. Coordinating the action between the release hand and the left eye, so that the release hand action comes before the left eye opens, will take practice. The left eye will assume major focus to see the arrow, while the head and bow can remain stationary. In this way the arrow flight line is protected by keeping the bow and head still, and at the same time the archer has

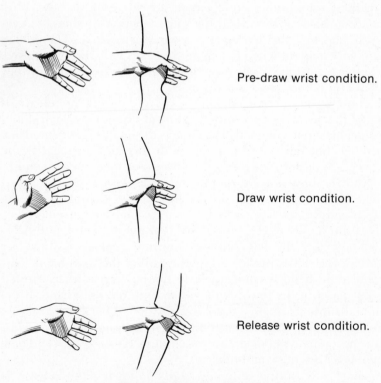

Pre-draw wrist condition.

Draw wrist condition.

Release wrist condition.

Three stages of a relaxed wrist.

the satisfaction of knowing where his arrow is landing. This is the one remedy that is approved as the best correction for peeking.

2. In some cases more drastic action is necessary. The next suggestion is a remedy which can be used temporarily or permanently depending on the archer's ability to perform. Keep both eyes open during the aim. For most archers this is very difficult, and so it is termed a drastic action. Perhaps, after shooting with both eyes open for a while, the archer can control peeking enough to go back to the first suggestion of opening the left eye on the release. When both eyes are open there are two factors of which the archer needs to be aware. The string alignment gets lost after the direct aiming begins, and can cause problems unless the muscles of the body stay in a very stationary position to lock in string alignment position. Sometimes during the aiming two golds appear. Always aim at the right gold!!! For most archers shooting with both eyes open is nearly impossible. Of course, this is not advocated as the best way of aiming. As a drastic cure for correcting a severe fault it can be used, hopefully as only a temporary measure.

PERFECTING THE FOLLOW-THROUGH

Thinking about shooting that last arrow and holding the final position of the release is the follow-through in archery. To perfect the follow-through means to hold it a little longer and to concentrate harder. An archer should maintain a shooting mood between arrows by holding a long follow-through and thinking about how the next arrow will be shot in perfect form. The follow-through technique is essential in making an archer independent on the shooting line. With time to analyze his performance, he has a chance of making corrections. He will not need another person with him constantly to tell him his faults. This independence pays off dividends in a tournament when the teacher or coach is not available. This self-sufficiency is good for the morale of the archer and very often sees him through competition crises.

PSYCHOLOGY OF COMPETITION IN ARCHERY

A successful archer is one who is analytical and methodical in his performance. A certain amount of "feel" is good, such as a feeling of rightness, comfort, ease, and physical well-being. To shoot by "feel" alone will not produce consistent scores, and so the archer must strive to be governed by concrete guide points he can rely on if he wishes to perform the same way every time. An archer becomes methodical and develops guide points through practice. Practice sessions should be devoted to technique, not the scoring of rounds. It may be more enjoyable to shoot for score, but practice for technique's sake will pay off in better scores when it really counts — in actual competition. Practice should be for good arrow groupings through the control of technique. Instead of the usual target face used for scoring, the archer should use a scrap of paper or an old scorecard as a target. In a good practice session an archer will be concerned only about how his technique affects his ability to group arrows on the target. As he manipulates his technique and consequently the arrow groupings, he is building a storehouse of knowledge for tournament competition. Any amount of this kind of invaluable information can be obtained only by good practice on the range. Practice sessions should be paced in content and length to suit the needs of a particular archer. The type of tournament for which he is preparing (distances to be shot and number of hours or days he will be shooting), his current physical condition, and his familiarity with the rounds to be shot, will determine what and how long his practice sessions should be. Pacing the practice to bring the archer to his peak just prior to a tournament is the goal. Throughout the practice periods, the archer develops confidence in himself and in his equipment. To go into a competitive event without this confidence is folly. A new bow does not build confidence as much as one that the archer knows. To "know" a bow is to understand its reaction, to be comfortable with its feel, to trust in its consistency of performance, and to know it has the potential of producing fantastic scores. While practicing with a bow an archer learns to handle it to its greatest effectiveness — soon archer and bow become united in a single goal of shooting arrows in the gold. This is confidence in one's equipment and it takes many hours of shooting for it to develop.

Concentration is the ability to close oneself off from outside factors. In archery there are many people close by during a tournament who might be distracting. There are also outside noises of cars or planes, and weather conditions of wind, cold, or heat which could annoy an archer. If an archer has the ability to concentrate while shooting his arrows, he will be unaware of or at least not annoyed by any outside factors. Only in this free environment of concentration will an archer perform his best.

Concentration must be practiced; it does not just happen. It takes discipline and perseverance on the part of the archer to develop his concentration powers. To concentrate in archery means to be completely and totally absorbed in how to shoot an arrow perfectly. Only thoughts of technique are in the mind. The depth of these thoughts will determine the quality of his concentration. An archer should be so deep in his thoughts that a jet plane going overhead creates very little disturbance. This power or ability is hard to achieve, but it is the goal of a tournament archer. The practice sessions should join together concentration practice as well as technique practice.

When trying to practice concentration, the archer is advised to formulate a thought pattern of technique sequence. He should become absorbed in stance, nock, draw, anchor, aim, and so forth, and should cover every detail that he knows will affect his arrow. Each archer will have his own method for checking his technique in each draw. In developing a thought pattern the archer mentally checks the quality of performance of each technique in a particular order. This thought pattern will assure him that nothing was left unchecked, and in time builds his self-confidence as well as his powers of concentration. A successful archer is a disciplined one. He is disciplined in the performance of technique, he has forced himself to be patient while learning new skills, and his emotions are under control so that fear, apprehension, excitement, anger, or annoyance will never manifest themselves to his detriment.

A positive attitude toward one's performance on any tournament day is essential for good shooting during that day. A negative attitude is a hindrance to the effort the archer might normally make. Tournament pressures which cause shattered nerves, uneven breathing, and queasy stomachs can be overcome if the archer has the power of concentration. He begins to close himself off by thinking of technique and forces himself to think more deeply. He does not dwell on the starting whistle, the number of contestants, or the awards that will be given out at the end of the tournament. He shoots one arrow at a time and is completely engrossed in making that one arrow perfect. The more nervous or upset he becomes the greater his efforts are to concentrate on his equipment or his technique. Concentration is the only combatant to tournament pressures. If the practice sessions were planned and executed well, you can rest assured the archer will enter a tournament well prepared.

Most collegiate archers at some time will shoot all or part of the F.I.T.A. round which is governed by the International Archery Federation rules. Following are excerpts the archer needs to know.

Conversion Table—Meters

	Yards	Feet	Inches
30 meters =	32	2	5.10
50 meters =	54	2	0.50
60 meters =	65	1	10.20
70 meters =	76	1	7.90
90 meters =	98	1	3.30

Archer's Equipment

This article (of the International Archery Federation rules) lays down the type of Equipment archers are permitted to use when shooting for F.I.T.A. purposes.

Items of Equipment not mentioned or covered in this Article are consequently not allowed to be used without prior approval of F.I.T.A. Congress. Further it will be necessary to place before Congress any Equipment or part thereof for which approval is requested.

a. A BOW of any type may be used provided it subscribes to the accepted principle and meaning of the word Bow as used in Target Archery: e.g. an instrument consisting of a handle (grip), riser and two flexible limbs each ending in a tip with a string nock.

   The Bow is braced for use by a single bowstring attached directly between the two string nocks only, and in operation is held in one hand by its handle (grip) while the fingers of the other hand draw, hold back and release the string.

b. A BOW STRING may be made up of any number of strands of the material chosen for the purpose, with a center serving to accommodate the drawing fingers, a nocking point to which may be added serving(s) to fit the arrow nock as necessary, and to locate this point one or two nock locators may be positioned, and in each of the two ends of the Bow String a loop to be placed in the string nocks of the Bow when braced. In addition one attachment, which may not exceed a diameter of one centimeter in any direction, is permitted on the String to serve as a lip or nose mark.

   A Bow String must not in any way offer aid in aiming through a peephole, marking or any other means.

c. AN ARROWREST, which can be adjustable, an ARROWPLATE and a DRAW CHECK INDICATOR may all be used on the Bow provided they are not electric or electronic and do not offer an additional aid in aiming.

d. A BOWSIGHT, BOWMARK or a POINT OF AIM on the ground for aiming are permitted, but at no time may more than one such device be used.

   (i) A BOWSIGHT as attached to the Bow for the purpose of aiming may allow for windage adjustment as well as elevation setting for aiming, but it is subject to the following provisions:

      It shall not incorporate a prism or lens or other magnifying device, leveling or electric devices nor shall it provide for more than one sighting point.

   (ii) A BOWMARK is a single mark made on the Bow for the purpose of aiming. Such mark may be made in pencil, tape or any other suitable marking material.

      A plate or tape with distance marking may be mounted on the Bow as a guide for marking, but must not in any way offer any additional aid.

   (iii) A POINT OF AIM on the ground is a marker placed in the shooting lane between the shooting line and the target. Such marker may not exceed a diameter of 7.5 cm and must not protrude above the ground more than 15 cm.

e. STABILIZERS on the Bow are permitted provided they do not:—

   (i) serve as a string guide

   (ii) touch anything but the Bow

(iii) represent any obstacle to other archers as far as place on the shooting line is concerned.

The numbers mounted shall not exceed four.

TORQUE FLIGHT COMPENSATORS (T.F.C.) may also be mounted.

f. ARROWS of any type may be used provided they subscribe to the accepted principle and meaning of the word Arrow as used in Target Archery, and that such Arrows do not cause undue damage to target faces and buttresses.

An Arrow consists of a nock, shaft and arrow head (point) with fletching and, if desired, cresting.

The Arrows of each archer shall be marked with the archer's name or insignia and shall have the same color(s) in fletching. If crested all Arrows shall carry the same pattern and color(s).

g. FINGER PROTECTIONS in the form of finger stalls or tips, gloves, shooting tab or tape (plaster) to draw, hold back and release the String are permitted, provided they are smooth with no device to help to hold and/or release the String.

A SEPARATOR between the fingers to prevent pinching may be used.

On the bow hand an ordinary glove, mitten or similar articles may be worn.

h. FIELD GLASSES, TELESCOPES and other visual aids may be used between shots for spotting arrows.

ORDINARY SPECTACLES as necessary or SHOOTING SPEC-TACLES provided they are fitted with the same lenses normally used by the archer, and SUN GLASSES. None must be fitted with micro-hole lenses, glasses or similar, nor marked in any way, which can assist in aiming.

i. ACCESSORIES are permitted such as bracers, dress shield, bowsling, belt or ground quiver, tassel; foot markers not protruding above the ground more than one centimeter.

Range Control and Safety

a. Under the control of the Field Captain, two ends of three sighter arrows are permitted preceding the commencement of shooting each day. No other trial shots are allowed, in any direction, on the shooting field during the days of any competition.

b. No archer may draw his bow, with or without an arrow, except when standing on the Shooting Line.

If an arrow is used, the archer shall aim towards the Targets but only after being satisfied that the field is clear both in front of and behind the Targets. If an archer, while drawing his bow with an arrow before the shooting starts or during breaks between distances, looses an arrow, intentionally or otherwise, such an arrow shall count as part of his quota of arrows for the distance to be shot, but shall not be scored, even if it hits his target.

c. While shooting is in progress, only those archers whose turn it is to shoot may be on the shooting line. All other archers with their tackle shall remain behind the waiting line. After an archer has shot his arrows, he shall retire behind the waiting line.

d. No archer may touch the tackle of another without the latter's consent.

e. An archer who arrives after shooting has started, shall forfeit the number of arrows already shot, unless the Field Captain is satisfied that he was delayed by circumstances beyond his control, in which case he may be allowed to make up the arrows lost after the distance then being shot has been completed.

Shooting

a. Each archer shall shoot his arrows in ends of three arrows each.
b. The maximum time permitted for an archer to shoot an end of three arrows shall be two and a half minutes. Any arrow not shot inside the Time Limit will be forfeited and any arrow shot in excess of this time will forfeit the highest scoring arrow for that end (of the 3 or 6 arrows as the case may be.) However, if it becomes necessary to change a string or make essential adjustment to equipment the Field Captain must be informed and extra time may be given.
c. Excepting for persons who are permanently disabled, archers shall shoot from a standing position and without support, with one foot on each side of the shooting line.
d. An arrow shall not be deemed to have been shot, if the archer can touch it with his bow without moving his feet from their position in relation to the shooting line.
e. While an archer is on the shooting line, he shall receive no assistance or information, by word or otherwise, from anyone, other than for the purpose of making essential changes in equipment.

Scoring

a. One Scorer shall be appointed for each target.
b. At 90, 70 and 60 meters, scoring shall take place after every second end (6 arrows) at World Championship Tournaments, but at other Tournaments scoring may take place after each end of 3 arrows or after every second end (6 arrows).
c. Scorers shall enter the value of each arrow on Score Sheets as called out by the Archers to whom the arrows belong. Other Archers on that target shall check the value of each arrow called out.
   Only arrows scoring ten points shall be referred to as "Golds."
d. Neither the arrows nor the face shall be touched until all the arrows on that target have been recorded.
e. An arrow shall be scored according to the position of the shaft in the target face.
f. If more than three arrows (or six as the case may be), belonging to same archer, should be found in the target or on the ground in the shooting lanes, only the three lowest (or six lowest, as the case may be) in value shall be scored. Should an archer be found to repeat this, he may be disqualified.
g. Should the shaft of an arrow touch two colors, or touch any dividing line between scoring zones, that arrow shall score the higher value of the zones affected.
h. Unless all arrow holes are suitably marked on each occasion when arrows are scored and drawn from the target, arrows rebounding from the target face shall not be scored.

i. An arrow hitting: —

   (i) The target and rebounding, shall score according to its point of impact on the target, provided that all arrow holes have been marked, and providing that an unmarked hole or mark made by the rebounding arrow can be identified. When a rebound occurs, the archer concerned will, after shooting his three arrows, remain on the shooting line with his bow held above his head as a signal to the Field Captain and Technical Commission. All other archers on the shooting line for that end will after shooting their three arrows retire behind the waiting line. The Field Captain will interrupt the shooting while a member of the Technical Commission together with the archer concerned or Team Captain if available will proceed to the target to judge the hit and take down the value of the rebound and mark the hole and later assist in the scoring for the archer concerned. The rebound arrow must be left behind the target until that end has been scored. The Field Captain will ensure the field is again clear and then give the signal for shooting to recommence.

   (ii) A target other than an archer's own target, shall not score.

   (iii) Another arrow in the nock and remaining embedded therein, shall score according to the value of the arrow struck.

   (iv) Another arrow, and then hitting the target face after deflection, shall score as it lies in the target.

   (v) Another arrow, and then rebounding from the target, shall score the value of the struck arrow, provided the damaged arrow can be identified.

   (vi) The target face after rebounding off the ground, shall not score.

Glossary

Address — Assuming the stance preparatory to shooting an arrow.

Alignment — Bow relationship to target; string relationship to bow as seen at anchor position.

Anchor point — A definite spot on the face with which the index finger of the string hand makes contact for consistency in shooting.

Archer's paradox — As the arrow leaves the bow it first deviates to the left (for a right-handed archer) and then stabilizes its flight by resuming a position directly in line with the center of the bow. The arrow actually bends around the bow.

Archery golf — The game of golf played with bow and arrow on a golf course.

Armguard — A leather protector for the inside of the bow forearm.

Arrowplate — A piece of leather shell or horn above the arrow rest where the arrow passes as it leaves the bow. An insert of hard material designed to protect the bow.

Arrow rest — A projection on the side of the bow on which the arrow rests. The part of the bow handle that forms a shelf.

Arrowsmith — A maker of metal arrowheads.

Ascham — A tall, narrow cabinet in which bows and arrows are kept.

Back — The part of the bow away from the archer.

Backed bow — One with a protection of material on the back; could be rawhide or fiberglass.

Balloon feather — A parabolic cut feather.

Barb — A projection on a hunting arrow head which prevents easy withdrawal.

Blunt — An arrow tip which is flat, used for small game hunting.

Bolt — A crossbow missile; also called dart.

Bow arm — The arm which supports the bow during shooting.

Bowman — An archer.

Bowsight — A mechanical device attached to the bow with which the archer can aim directly at the target.

Bow stave — A piece of wood from which a bow is made.

Bow strap — A leather strap attached to the bow that allows the archer's hand to remain in contact with the bow without holding.

Bow window — The cut out section above the grip in a wood bow; also called sight window; centershoot.

Bowyer — A bow maker.

Bracer — An armguard; a device for stringing (bracing) a bow.

Bracing — To string a bow; to place loops of string into the bow nocks.

Broadhead — A broad sharply pointed arrowhead used for hunting.

Brush button — A soft gum rubber object placed at each end of the bowstring to eliminate bow noise; a form of silencer used in bow hunting.

Butt — A backstop for arrows; a target; a matt; a bale of hay.

Cast — The speed and distance a bow can propel an arrow.

Chrysal — A fracture of the fibers in a bow that shows as a line across the belly of the bow.

Clicker — A metal device attached to the side of the bow above the arrow rest that acts as a draw check. The arrow is placed under the metal strip in the nocking stage. After the entire arrow is drawn the metal strip "clicks" against the bow notifying the archer that his arrow has been completely drawn.

Clout — Long-distance type of shooting which uses a 48-foot target which is flat on the ground.

Cock feather — The odd colored feather situated at right angles to the nock.

Composite bow — A bow made of two or more kinds of material.

Creeping — The edging forward of the fully drawn arrow just prior to the release.

Crest — Identifying markings on the arrow — usually bands close to the vanes.

Dead release — Releasing the string by allowing the string fingers to move toward the target.

Draw — To spread the bow.

Draw check — Determining the amount of arrow drawn for each shot.

Drawing fingers — The middle three fingers of the string hand.

Drift — The drift to either side (windage) due to a cross wind.

Elevation — Height of the bowhand while aiming.

End — Six arrows shot consecutively.

Eye — Loop(s) of the string.

Field captain — Man in charge of a tournament.

Finger tab — A small piece of leather used to protect the three drawing fingers.

Finger sling — A leather strip with a loop at either end that enables an archer to hold the bow loosely by inserting his thumb and index fingers of the bowhand into these loops.

Fletcher — An arrow maker.

Fletching — The feathers on an arrow that guide and stabilize the arrow in flight.

Flight — Course of an arrow after leaving the bow; distance shooting.

Flight compensator — Metal object placed under the stabilizers that counteracts any fault causing torque.

Flinch — A sudden body movement caused by indecision when in a full draw: to release or not to release.

Flirt — An arrow that jumps out of its line of flight.

Flu flu — Spiral feathering on an arrow used for wing shooting.

Follow-through — Holding the release position in order to insure direction and accurate flight to the arrow.

Footed arrow — An arrow that has an insert of hardwood in the pile end for strength and added weight.

Gold — Center of the target.

Grip — Handle of the bow.

Grouping — A cluster of arrows that have been shot; a close group.

Handle — The grip of the bow.

Hanging arrow — An arrow which has penetrated the target with the pile (tip) only and hangs across the target face.

Head — The tip, point or pile of the arrow.

Hen feathers — The two feathers on either side of the cock feather.

Hit — A successful shot.

Holding — Holding an arrow at full draw while aiming; to steady down.

Jig — A device for putting feathers on the arrow; one for making strings.

Jointed bow — A two piece bow; a take down bow; a carriage bow.

Kick — Recoil of the bow during the release.

Kiss button — Any device attached to the string that will contact the lips when in the correct anchor position; an additional contact point to insure consistency of the draw.

Lady paramount — Woman in charge of a tournament.

Laminated bow — A layered bow made of several materials.

Level — A small fluid level (1 inch) attached to the bow that will aid the archer in maintaining a true vertical bow position.

Limbs — The arms of a bow; upper and lower ends.

Loose — The act of releasing the string.

Match — A competitive event usually by mail or telegraph.

Midnock — A nock which is tapered down from the base to the groove. It gives a smoother release.

Mis-nock — When the arrow falls out of the bow on the release instead of flying to the target. This occurs when the string is not in the nock of the arrow at the moment of release.

NAA — National Archery Association.

NFAA — National Field Archery Association.

Nock — The groove at the end of the arrow into which the string is placed; the technique of placing the arrow into the bow preparatory to shooting.

Nocking point — A specific spot on the string where the arrow is placed for each shot.

Open stance — A position of the body which is opened to the target.

Overbowed — An archer who is drawing too strong a bow.

Overdraw — To draw the arrow beyond the inside face of the bow; to pull a bow beyond its limits.

Overshoot — To shoot beyond the goal.

Overstrung — When the string is too short for the bow — the string height is too great.

Peeking — The act of looking at the arrow in flight or landing. This is a fault that hinders good scoring.

Peep sight — A small aperture placed into the string that lines up with the aiming eye. It acts as a hind sight.

Petticoat — The edge of the target outside the scoring area.

Pile — The tip, head, or point of the arrow.

Pinching — Squeezing the nock of the arrow during the draw.

Plastic vanes — Those made of plastic that are weather- and wind-proof.

Plucking — Snapping the release hand away and to the side of the face.

Point blank — When the aim and the flight follow the same path.

Prism — A sighting device which refracts the sight line thereby giving a clear view of the target. It is available in various degrees of refraction.

Quiver — Any receptacle to hold the arrow; ground, hip or back quivers.

Range — The distance to be shot; the place where shooting takes place.

Rebound — An arrow that hits the scoring face and rebounds forward.

Recurved bow — The reverse curves on a bow.

Reflexed bow — A bow that bends backwards when unstrung.

Release — To allow the string to roll off the fingers and thereby propel the arrow.

Riser — The center part of the bow that includes the handle; usually heavier and more massive than the limbs.

Round — A prescribed number of ends at a prescribed distance.

Roving — Shooting at random targets, usually in a wooded area.

Scatter — Opposite of grouping; arrows in different places on the target.

Self — Bow or arrows made from a single piece of wood.

Serving—The thread reinforcement on the center of the string opposite the grip.

Shaft—The main portion of the arrow; the body of the arrow.

Shooting line—A line indicating a specific distance on the range.

Six golds—A perfect end.

Snake—An arrow snakes when it disappears under the turf of the grass.

Speednock—One which has a molded index on top of the nock to locate the cock feather by feel.

Spine—The strength, resiliency, and flexibility of the arrow which must match the power of thrust (weight) of the bow.

Spiral—The curved or angled position that feathers occupy on the shaft.

Spot—The aiming center of a black and white target face.

Stabilizer—Additional weights at each end of riser which help to eliminate torque and to absorb the shock of the release.

Stacking—The rapid increase of weight during the last few inches of draw.

Tackle—Archery equipment.

Target captain—An archer in charge of a target; one who calls score and pulls arrows.

Target face—Scoring area.

Timber—Equivalent to "Fore" in golf; a warning in field shooting that an arrow is being shot.

Torque—A twisting action in the bow as a result of the bow hand or wrist turning left or right on the release.

Toxophilite—A student of archery; an archer.

Toxophilus—The first archery book, written by Roger Ascham in 1544.

Trajectory—The path of an arrow in flight.

Twisted limb—The extreme end of the limb is not in line with the main portion of the bow. This is caused by improper bracing or storage.

Underbowed—A bow which has a string too long, resulting in too narrow a string height.

Vane—Feather of an arrow.

Wand—A narrow stick used as a target.

Weight—The total pull required to spread a bow completely which is measured in pounds; the weight of an arrow in grams.

Whip ended—When the limbs of the bow are too weak at the tips.

Wide—The flight of the arrow to either side of target; to be wide of the mark.

Windage—Left-right variation in the arrow flight.

Wobble—Erratic action of an arrow in flight.

Selected References

Burke, Edmund: *The History of Archery*. New York, William Morrow and Co., 1957.
A comprehensive account of the known history of archery; a reference of invaluable information.

Division of Girls and Women's Sports: *Archery-Riding Guide*. Washington, D.C., AAHPER., 1201 16th st., N.W. Published every two years (1970-1972 current issue).
A booklet containing information on all phases of archery, teaching methods, equipment, safety, competition, and rules. Invaluable source of information.

Keaggy, David J., Sr.: *Power Archery*. Riderwood, Maryland, Archery World Magazine 1964 (First Edition).
An explanation of a style of shooting as originated by David Keaggy. Excellent in content and for the in-depth study of archery technique.

Keaggy, David J., Sr.: *Power Archery*. Drayton Plains, Michigan, Power Archery Products, 1968 (Second Edition).
An updated version of the first book written by David Keaggy. A deeper analysis of archery technique than the previous edition.

Klann, Margaret: *Target Archery*. Reading, Massachusetts, Addison-Wesley Publishing Co., 1970.
An excellent archery text for the archery teacher and physical education major. The whole treatment of archery, from technique of shooting and physiological aspects of shooting to the quality of illustrations, makes this book indispensable.

National Archery Association: *The Archer's Handbook*. Ronks, Pennsylvania, Clayton Shenk, 2833 Lincoln Highway East. 1968.
A compilation of archery information needed for running a tournament, establishing a club, and so forth.

RULE BOOKS

The Division of Girls and Women's Sports: *Archery-Riding Guide*. Washington, D.C., AAHPER, 1201 16th St., N.W. Published every two years.

The National Archery Association: *Official Tournament Rules*. Revised as needed. 2833 Lincoln Highway E., Ronks, Pennsylvania.

MAGAZINES

Archery World. Archery Associates, Inc. Box 124, Boyerstown, Pennsylvania. Monthly. Official publication of the National Archery Association.

Bow and Arrow. Gallant Publishing Co. 116 E. Badillo, Covina, California. Bimonthly.

Archery Magazine. P.O. Box H, Palm Springs, California. Monthly. Official publication of the National Field Archery Association.